Triune Books

AMERICAN FURNITURE

AMERICAN FURNITURE
from the first Colonies to World War 1

Joseph T. Butler

ACKNOWLEDGMENTS

(page 1)
Butterfly table
Jacobean, New England, maple,
1700–1730. *New Hampshire
Historical Society*

(page 3)
Brewster-type arm chair
Jacobean, New England, oak,
1650–1675. *Henry Ford Museum*

ISBN 0 85674 011 X
Published 1973 by
Triune Books, London, England
Printed in Spain by
Printer, Industria Gráfica S.A. Tuset 19
Barcelona, San Vicente dels Horts 1973
Depósito legal B. 18972-1973
Mohn Gordon Ltd. London

The publishers gratefully acknowledge the following, who have
supplied the illustrations for this book:
Albany Institute of History and Art: 24*b*, 92*tl*, 102*t*, 113*l*. The
American Museum in Britain, Bath: 12*br*, 32, 40*b*, 43, 73*l*, 98, 103*b*,
112*br*, 117*t*, 122, 128. The Art Institute of Chicago: 82. The
Baltimore Museum of Art: Gift of Lydia Howard deRoth and
Nancy H. deFord Venable 95*b*, 96. The Brooklyn Museum: 14*t*,
38, 67, 106*t*, 111*t*, 119*t*; Gift of Miss Gwendolin O. L. Conkling
126. Chicago Historical Society: 132*b*. Colonial Williamsburg: 19*c*,
26*t*. The Currier Gallery of Art, Manchester, New Hampshire: 60*r*.
Essex Institute, Salem, Massachusetts: 88*r*. Hancock Shaker Village:
125*b*. Henry Ford Museum, Dearborn, Michigan: 1, 20, 121, 125*t*,
131. Henry Francis duPont Winterthur Museum, Delaware: 8*t*, *b*,
10*t*, 12*t*, 25*r*, 28*t*, *b*, 29, 30*t*, *b*, 31, 33*t*, *b*, 35*tr*, 36*l*, *r*, 37*l*, *r*, 39, 40*t*,
41*tl*, *tr*, *b*, 42, 45, 47*t*, 48*l*, *r*, 49*l*, 50*l*, 51*tl*, *b*, 52*t*, *b*, 53*tl*, *tr*, *bl*, *br*,
54*l*, *r*, 55*t*, *bl*, *br*, 56*l*, *r*, 57*l*, *r*, 58*t*, *b*, 59, 60*l*, 61*l*, *r*, 62, 63, 64*t*, 65*l*,
tr, *br*, 66, 68*t*, *bl*, *br*, 69*l*, *r*, 70*t*, *b*, 71*tl*, *tr*, *b*, 72*tl*, *bl*, *r*, 76*t*, *b*, 77*t*, *b*,
80, 85, 91*l*, *r*, 92*bl*, *r*, 93*l*, *r*, 95*t*, 100*t*, 109*t*, *b*, 111*b*, 113*tr*, 120, 124*bl*.
Horizon Press, New York: 143*t*. Houston Museum of Fine Arts:
Bayou Bend Collection 51*tr*, 89*t*, 101*b*, 114*t*. The Metropolitan
Museum of Art: 15*r*, 16*b*, 22*br*, 24*t* and detail, 27, 35*b*, 46, 78, 88*l*,
89*b*, 99, 113*br*, 143*b*, 144*t*; Anonymous Fund Gift 141; Bequest of
Herbert Lee Pratt 21*l*; Bequest of Mrs Maria P. James 108*b*; Edgar
J. Kaufmann Charitable Foundation Fund 112*tr*, 124*tl*, 129*t*, 134,
144*b*; Gift of Paul Martini 142*t*; Gift of Mrs J. Insley Blair 13*t*, 17;
Gift of Mrs Russell Sage and others 107; Gift of Mrs Florence
Weyman 138; Gift of John C. Cattus 112*l*; Gift of Mrs William W.
Hoppin 124*r*; Gift of Charles Tisch 127; Gift of Mrs Charles
Reginald Leonard 133; Gift of Mrs D. Chester Noyes 135*t*; Gift of
Josephine M. Fiala 136; Gift of Mary J. Kingsland 137; Joseph
Pulitzer Bequest 23*l*; Purchase, Mrs Paul Moore Gift 115*t*; Purchase
Fund, L. E. Katzenbach Gift 115*b*; Rogers Fund 132*t*. Museum of
the City of New York: 22*t*, 129*br*, 135*c*. Museum of Early Southern
Decorative Arts, Winston Salem, North Carolina: 75, 106*b*, 110*t*.
Museum of Fine Arts, Boston: 11; Gift of Mrs Horatio A. Lamb
110*b*; M. and M. Karolik Collection 44, 84*r*, 87, 94*l*, *r*, 97*t*, *b*, 100*b*,
101*t*, 103*t*, 118*t*. National Gallery of Art: Gift of Edgar William and
Bernice Chrysler Garbisch 79. The National Trust for Historic
Preservation, Washington, DC: 118*b*. New Hampshire Historical
Society, Concord: 3, 26*b*; Prentis Collection 9*b*. The New York
Historical Society 114*b*, 119*b*, 123. The Old Gaol Museum, York,
Maine 35*tl*. Park District of Oak Park, Illinois 142*b*. Philadelphia
Museum of Art: 50*r*, 73*r*, 74, 81*r*, 90*l*, *r*, 116, 117*b*. Sagamore Hill,
Oyster Bay, New York: 140*t*. Sleepy Hollow Restorations,
Tarrytown, New York: 14*bl*, *br*, 19*t*, *b*, 21*r*, 34, 47*b*, 49*r*, 56*c*, 64*b*,
83, 105, 108*t*, 129*bl*, 135*b*, 139*t*, *b*; Loan from Mr and Mrs Mitchell
Taradish 23*r*. Smithsonian Institution, Washington, DC:
Greenwood Gift 9*t*, 15*l*, 16*t*, 18, 140*b*. Society for the
Preservation of New England Antiquities: 102*b*. Wadsworth
Atheneum, Hertford, Connecticut: Nutting Collection 22*bl*. Yale
University Art Gallery, New Haven, Connecticut: Gift of Charles
Betts 12*bl*; The Mabel Brady Garvan Collection 13*b*, 81*l*, 85*l*.

CONTENTS

page 6 Preface

7 Reading List

8 Origins of furniture making in America

10 Styles of the 17th century

20 The William and Mary style 1700–1725

28 The Queen Anne style 1725–1755

43 The Chippendale style 1755–1785

84 Classical styles 1785–1850

130 Other revival styles 1830–1900

139 Innovation and reform 1850–1914

Preface

It is hoped that this small volume will be of general interest to those who wish to learn about American furniture. The Reading List (opposite page) includes many of the standard works on the subject, both general and specialized, and offers an opportunity for further exploration of the field. It is not intended as a connoisseurship guide or as a definitive history of the subject. Rather, it is a step-by-step examination of the manner in which furniture styles have evolved in America.

The illustrations are included as an important adjunct to the text. Their arrangement generally follows the stylistic development discussed. In some instances, pieces from such closely related styles as the Queen Anne and Chippendale are shown in juxtaposition so that their evolution can be seen more easily. Sometimes groups of individual furniture forms are shown together so that the regional characteristics might be distinguished. Elaborate urban pieces are shown with simplified country examples which were being produced at the same time.

It is hoped that this visual experience will be of help to the reader.

Many institutions in the United States, and one in England, have provided illustrative material without which the book would not have been possible. I gratefully acknowledge here my indebtedness to the staffs of these institutions.

Joseph T. Butler
Dobbs Ferry, New York

Reading List

General

Ethel Hall Bjerkoe	*The Cabinetmakers of America*, Garden City (NY) 1957
Helen Comstock	*American Furniture*, New York, 1962
Helena Hayward	(Ed.) *World Furniture*, New York—Toronto, 1965
John T. Kirk	*Early American Furniture*, New York, 1970
Luke Vincent Lockwood	*The Furniture Collectors' Glossary*, New York, 1913
Edgar G. Miller	*American Furniture*, New York, 1950
Wallace Nutting	*Furniture Treasury*, (3 vol.), New York, 1948
Albert Sack	*Fine Points of Furniture—Early American*, New York, 1950
Ole Wanscher	*The Art of Furniture*, New York, 1966

Specialized

American Heritage	*History of Colonial Antiques*, New York, 1967
American Heritage	*History of American Antiques from the Revolution to the Civil War*, New York, 1968
American Heritage	*History of Antiques from the Civil War to World War I*, New York, 1969
Baltimore Museum of Art	*Baltimore Furniture, 1760–1810*, Baltimore, 1947
Baltimore Museum of Art	*Maryland Queen Anne and Chippendale Furniture of the Eighteenth Century*, Baltimore, 1968
E. Milby Burton	*Charleston Furniture 1700–1825*, Charleston, 1955
Joseph T. Butler	*American Antiques 1800–1900*, New York, 1965
Helen Comstock	*The Looking Glass in America 1700–1825*, New York, 1968
Charles Over Cornelius	*Furniture Masterpieces of Duncan Phyfe*, New York, 1923
Currier Gallery of Art	*The Dunlaps and their Furniture*, Manchester (NH), 1970
Joseph Downs	*American Furniture Queen Anne and Chippendale Periods*, New York, 1952
William Voss III Elder	*Baltimore Painted Furniture 1800–1840*, Baltimore, 1972
Dean Fales, Jr.	*American Painted Furniture 1660–1880*, New York, 1972
Wendell D. Garrett Paul F. Norton Alan Gowans Joseph T. Butler	*The Arts in America The Nineteenth Century*, New York, 1969
Marion Day Iverson	*The American Chair 1630–1890*, New York, 1957
Russell Haines Kettell	*Pine Furniture of Early New England*, Garden City (NY), 1929
John T. Kirk	*American Chairs: Queen Anne and Chippendale*, New York, 1972
Luke Vincent Lockwood	*Colonial Furniture in America*, (2 vols.), New York, 1913
Nancy McClelland	*Duncan Phyfe and the English Regency, 1795–1830*, New York, 1939
Metropolitan Museum of Art	*19th Century America—Furniture and Decorative Arts*, New York, 1970
Charles Montgomery	*American Furniture The Federal Period*, New York, 1966
Celia Jackson Otto	*American Furniture of the Nineteenth Century*, New York, 1965
Wadsworth Atheneum	*Connecticut Furniture Seventeenth and Eighteenth Centuries*, Hartford, 1967
Peter Ward-Jackson	*English Furniture Designs of the Eighteenth Century*, London, 1958
Louis B. Wright: George B. Tatum: John N. McCoubrey, C. Robert	*The Arts in America, The Colonial Period*, New York, 1966

Origins of furniture making in America

Graduated slat-back chair
Jacobean, New Jersey, Maple,
c. 1710. *The Henry F. duPont
Winterthur Museum*

Chest of drawers
Jacobean, Ipswich, Massachusetts,
oak and other woods painted, 1678
(dated). *The Henry F. duPont
Winterthur Museum*

The origins of furniture making in America during the 17th century are to be found in the training and knowledge of colonists who brought with them the memory of styles with which they had been familiar in Europe. As the colonists came from different countries, it was only natural that the American-made furniture would be reminiscent of the style and tradition of that country. Thus, 17th century New England furniture has a strong English flavor while that made in New York has Dutch baroque style and form.

Native American woods were used in place of the more popular European woods. Wood was much more plentiful in America than in Europe but iron was much less so. The earliest tools in use were brought with the colonists but they were quick to produce such items. These differences among the colonial craftsmen, plus the influence of the new world, caused a phenomenon to develop in the character of American furniture, so that often it can be identified with its region of origin. Regional characteristics vary from one area to another and it is through these that source identification can be made. By the middle of the 18th century, these characteristics became highly developed and it is possible to distinguish, to a fine degree, the work of several east coast centers of furniture making. Regional characteristics remained an important aspect of American furniture until the end of the first quarter of the 19th century, when a number of different circumstances combined to cause them to disappear.

The term 'furniture making' has been used so far in a comprehensive sense. Actually, it can be divided generally into two parts—cabinetmaking and joinery. Cabinetmaking is the regulated trade which produced fine furniture. The cabinetmaker usually served an apprenticeship through which he became familiar with design and style as well as the use of, sophisticated tools. A fine piece of furniture produced in a good cabinetshop commonly followed the popular style of the day. In Europe, this would be the style of a court or monarch and it was these styles which were

Fourteen-panel chest
Jacobean, probably Massachusetts,
oak, c. 1680. *Smithsonian
Institution*

Arm chair
Late William and Mary, New
Hampshire, upholstered over pine
frame, 1690–1710. *New Hampshire
Historical Society*

eventually to filter to the colonies. Joined furniture
was less style-conscious. The joiner was not as well
trained as the cabinetmaker; the lathe was one of his
chief tools. As a rule, this furniture has a number of
turned members (parts) which are pinned together.
It sometimes does not follow the current high style
and is derivative of one which was popular at an
earlier time. Joined furniture can, in part, be associated
with rural areas and is termed 'country' or 'primitive',
but it should be kept in mind that the joiner also
operated in urban areas.

Because of the extended time involved in transpor-
tation and communication, American colonial styles
were at first behind those of Europe. However, as the
travelling time between Europe and America was
lessened, so was the style lag. The earliest cabinetmakers and joiners undoubtedly brought with them
only a remembrance of furniture which they had
made and seen. Fine cabinet shops in Europe owned
design books which pictured the popular style of the
day. Plates in these books showed furniture which the
shop might produce. Such books were also handy for
the patron because they enabled him to show the
cabinetmaker details which he wished to have incorporated in the piece he was commissioning. It is
not known when the first furniture design book
reached America, but it was not until the 18th century.

Thus, two important factors—heredity and en-
vironment—were to be of great importance in
founding the style and character of American
furniture. At its best and most original, it is still
derivative of the proportion and ornamentation of
European styles, but the use of new woods and elim-
ination of superfluous detail sometimes elevate it to a
position of unique beauty and design.

9

Styles of the 17th century

Book or desk box
Jacobean, probably Massachusetts, white and red oak with traces of paint, 1650–1680. *The Henry F. duPont Winterthur Museum*

In contrast to Europe, the development of a proper terminology for furniture styles in America is relatively difficult. In Europe, the style is generally called after the name of a reigning monarch. This will not always totally suffice for American furniture because of the time lag in transmission of style; also, styles from different countries simultaneously influenced their particular colonial areas of settlement. Style terminology in America has developed with a use of the names of English monarchs plus those of particular furniture designers. It is understood that the periods based on reigns do not coincide in terms of time with those in Europe.

The two earliest American colonies were Jamestown (1607) and Plymouth (1620). When they were founded James I (reigned 1603–1625) was on the throne of England. For this reason, the term Jacobean is often used to describe the earliest American furniture. At this time northern Europe had not completely emerged from the Middle Ages. The influence of Italian Renaissance design was beginning to reach England. During the 16th century, probably by way of Flanders, classic elements began to appear in English furniture design. Linen-fold patterns began to be replaced by arcaded panels and heavy bulbous feet and legs were introduced on furniture. Strapwork, the interweaving of geometric and scrolled bands, also appeared in carving. This Flemish influence probably came through design books and the migration of Flemish-Huguenot craftsmen. They communicated Renaissance design to a somewhat backward England and it was these designs and their resultant style which was transplanted to America. Early books on the history of American furniture have referred to this earliest period as 'Pilgrim'. The term is avoided here as the designation properly refers to a highly limited amount of furniture made by a very small group.

Oak was the chief wood used in furniture of this period. This heavy, durable wood well suited the Renaissance character of the furniture—which can best be described as massive, sturdy and rectilinear.

The most imposing form produced during this period in America was the court or press cupboard, see page 12, used for the storage of food and household goods as well as for the display of silver and other important possessions. The court cupboard has a cabinet with doors above and an open shelf below, while the press cupboard has a cabinet both above and

Press cupboard
Jacobean, Massachusetts, Essex County, oak and pine with ebonization, 1680–1700. *Museum of Fine Arts, Boston*

Court cupboard
Jacobean, Massachusetts, oak, 1684
(date inscribed on front). *The Henry
F. duPont Winterthur Museum*

Press cupboard
Jacobean, Connecticut,
Wethersfield-Hartford area, oak
with ebonization, 1670–1710. *Yale
University Art Gallery*

(right)
Chest over drawers
Jacobean, Connecticut, Hartford
County, oak, 1670–1690 and
Elbow chair
New England, maple and hickory,
1675–1700. Both *The American
Museum in Britain, Bath*

below. Decoration for these pieces was provided by applied ornament, which was often ebonized (painted black) to simulate the rich effect of ebony which was popular in Europe. Split spindles were often applied this way, as were bosses or jewels (small oval rounded pieces of wood). Closely related to the court and press cupboard was the chest. Sometimes chests were simple boxes composed of six boards and, if decorated, incorporated chip or scratch carving.

Three important types of chests are associated with Connecticut during the time. The Hadley chest, often of oak and pine, was made in the Connecticut Valley during the second half of the century. It is decorated with flat-carved leaves and scrolls and often bears the initials of the original owner. Over 100 examples of this type of chest are known today. At the same time, the 'sunflower' chest was being produced around Hartford. It received its name from the flat-carved sunflowers found in the panels. The final type, the Guilford chest, was painted with flowers and vines. These early low chests sometimes had a drawer or two at the bottom and it is from this form that the blanket chest evolved. It stands higher, has two or three

Chest of drawers
Jacobean, William and Mary,
probably New England, oak,
c. 1690. *The Metropolitan Museum
of Art*

Blanket chest
Jacobean, south central Connecticut,
oak with ebonization, 1670–1710.
Yale University Art Gallery

drawers and a storage compartment at the top with a lift lid, see page 13. Near the end of the century, the first true chests of drawers began to develop. These were supported on ball feet or the sides of the chest continued to the floor. Another rare, related form is the chest-on-frame, which consists of a box or small chest mounted on a turned frame. Pieces of this type are generally painted, sometimes with bright colors.

It might be said that all of the furniture produced at this time was joined; more sophisticated cabinet-making had not yet been introduced. Joinery can be studied in the chair forms which were produced at the time. These are generally divided into two types and given the names Brewster, and Carver. The specific chairs for which the types are named are at Pilgrim Hall, Plymouth, Massachusetts. Brewster chairs,

(above)
Chest on frame
Jacobean, Massachusetts, oak, pine and maple with paint, c. 1700. *The Brooklyn Museum*

(right)
Arm chair
William and Mary, New York, Hudson River Valley, pine and maple, painted c. 1695. *Sleepy Hollow Restorations*

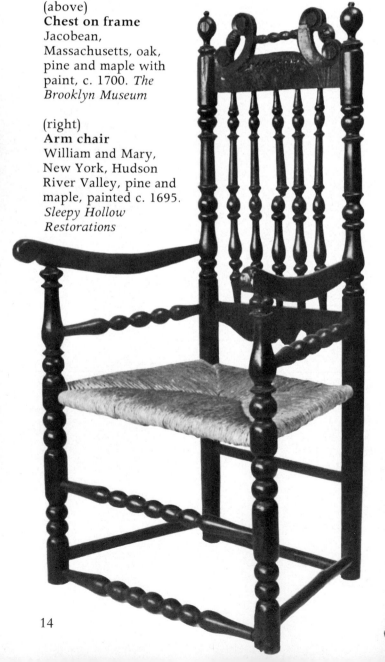

Side Chair
William and Mary—Queen Anne, New York, Hudson River Valley, stamped 'D. Coutong', maple with rush seat, c. 1740. *Sleepy Hollow Restorations*

Slat-back arm chair
Jacobean, New England, oak, 1691
(scratched on back of upper slat).
Smithsonian Institution

Joint stool
Jacobean, probably New England,
cherry, 1700–1725. *The
Metropolitan Museum of Art*

named after the elder William Brewster (1567–1644)
of the Plymouth colony, are those with spindles under
the arms and sometimes under the seat. Carver
chairs, for John Carver (died 1621), first governor of
the Plymouth colony, have spindles only in the back.
The wainscot chair was made only in the earliest
years of settlement. It had a paneled back and solid
wooden seat; sometimes the back panel was elaborately flat-carved. Slat-back chairs began to be made
at this time. The back is composed of a series of slats
arranged as a ladder which popularly has given them
their name. The early examples have a heaviness
which approximates that of Brewster and Carver

15

chairs, while later examples tend to be lighter. This type of stick furniture has continued to be made, with only slight modification, until the present day. Woods such as ash, elm, hickory, and maple were often combined in this type of furniture.

Tables were of two general types and can be characterized by the kind of support used as either trestle or stretcher. They were made in many sizes and often have bold turnings. The gateleg table is of the stretcher type with two drop leaves which can be supported by turned 'gates', as is the butterfly table which has drop leaves supported by wing-shaped

members, see page 3. Joint or joined stools are smaller but constructed like the stretcher table. They were one of the principal forms of seat furniture in late 17th century rooms although they are stylistically related to the table in form. The name 'form' for the joint stool is sometimes found in old inventories. Certain relatively original types were developed at this time to save space: the chair-table with tilt top could be used for either purpose, see page 18. Folding beds could be placed against the wall when not in use—each of these combined elements of convertibility and movability suitable to the multi-purpose room.

Folding table
Jacobean, Massachusetts, Essex County, oak and maple with marbelizing, 1675–1700. *The Metropolitan Museum of Art*

Chair table
Jacobean, probably Connecticut, oak, 1650–1675. *Smithsonian Institution*

18

Documents of the 17th century have revealed little information about American joiners. Thomas Dennis is generally regarded as the earliest maker about whom there is some body of knowledge. He was born in England c. 1630 and must have been trained there as a joiner and carver. Dennis is recorded as having been in Portsmouth, New Hampshire in 1663 and Ipswich, Massachusetts in 1688. He worked in the Jacobean style and is chiefly remembered as a maker of chests, court cupboards, and wainscot chairs. The estate inventory of Nicholas Disbrowe (1612/13–1683) shows that he owned many joiner's tools and the documentation concerning Governor John Winthrop's wainscot chair (Wesleyan University, Middletown, Connecticut) established it as his work. He has often been associated with the Hartford (sunflower) chest, but more recent research has assigned the chests to another maker, Peter Blin of Wethersfield, Connecticut, who was active between 1675 and 1725. Two families of cabinetmakers are associated with the Hadley chest: John Allis (1645–1691) and Samuel Belding (1633–1713) were followed by their sons Ichabod Allis (1675–1747) and Samuel Belding, Jr (1657–1737). Another cabinetmaker, John Hawkes (born 1643), is associated with this group.

The problem of dating furniture from this period is especially difficult. Documentary evidence is scant and inscribed dates, which can be trusted as accurate, are almost non-existent. Therefore, dating should be approached with great care and it can be assumed that most surviving examples date from the second half of the century. Although it began to be supplanted by the William and Mary at the end of the century, pieces in the earlier tradition continued to be made. The interiors into which this furniture was incorporated were relatively uncomfortable. Ceilings were low and paneling, if any, consisted of sheathing. Windows were small, so that the room was dark and the fire from the large hearth was welcomed for heat and light. Rushes or animal skins were the only relief to the chill of the bare floor. Inventories reveal that the furniture in these all purpose rooms was sparse. The two-room Hart House (Ipswich, Mass.) built c. 1640 typifies this type of interior, see page 35. The rooms may now be seen installed (one each) at the Henry Francis duPont Winterthur Museum, and the American Wing, The Metropolitan Museum of Art.

Gate-leg table
Jacobean, William and Mary, New York, mahogany and cherry, c. 1690. *Sleepy Hollow Restorations*

Table
William and Mary, possibly South Carolina, tulip and pine, 1700–1725. *Colonial Williamsburg*

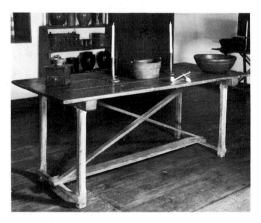

Stretcher-base table
Jacobean, William and Mary, New York, Hudson River Valley, pine with paint, c. 1740. *Sleepy Hollow Restorations*

The William and Mary style 1700—1725

The accession of William and Mary to the throne of England in 1689 created new links between England and the continent. This reign lasted until William's death in 1702 and was marked not only by the adoption of many Dutch traditions but through the actual importation of Dutch courtiers and craftsmen. England thus ceased to be the provincial island she once had been and more rapidly assimilated the tastes of continental Europe.

English taste of the period might be typified as Anglo-Dutch and inspiration was drawn from the Italian baroque as well as the court of Louis XIV. Furniture contained elaborate turned members, severe curves, high relief carving, large unified shapes and contrasts of color. From the Orient, caning and japanning or the imitation of lacquer were adopted. An original contribution was made by England in the form of case furniture with simple flat surfaces and architectural trim. This was to be the chief influence on Anglo-American case furniture for over a century.

(left)
Spanish foot side chair
William and Mary, New England, walnut painted black, 1700–1720.
Henry Ford Museum

(opposite)
Scroll foot side chair
William and Mary, New York, maple, beech and cane, c. 1690.
The Metropolitan Museum of Art

At the beginning of the 18th century, the American home began to reflect a greater comfort as well as a simple version of baroque taste. Turnings related in shape to Oriental vases began to be used in tables as well as interior architectural elements. Also introduced was a tapering scrolled foot which has long been called the Spanish foot. In reality, it would seem to have had its origins in Portugal and was brought to England during the reign of Charles II (1660–1685). In chairs, the curved elements of the cresting piece reflected the influence of Chinese design as well as the designs of Daniel Marot, a Huguenot designer employed by William and Mary.

More elaborate pieces of case furniture began to develop. The chest of drawers was sometimes combined with an upper section to form a secretary desk. A fall-front was generally included and the piece rested on bun feet. An important early survival is the fall-front writing cabinet now preserved at Colonial Williamsburg, signed by the maker Edward Evans of Pennsylvania and dated 1707. It is made of walnut,

(right)
Slope-front desk
William and Mary, New York, maple with walnut-burl veneer, 1690–1710. *Sleepy Hollow Restorations*

which was the popular fashion in Pennsylvania, while in New England maple and pine were used, often with walnut veneers. The bun feet and heavy cornices of these case pieces are reflections of their Anglo-Dutch design origin. Sometimes, table-like bases were combined with drawers and this brought about the development of the dressing table (lowboy). Tall versions of these were made (highboys), sometimes as companions to the dressing table. These forms were to persist through most of the 18th century, and were to show the changes of style.

Trumpet-turned or baroque-cupped legs characterize these case pieces. Their surfaces were enriched by textured and grained veneers in walnut and maple. In other instances, japanning, in imitation of popular Oriental lacquers, was used, see opposite. Here chinoiserie elements were set against a black background;

(top)
Secretary
William and Mary, New York, walnut, c. 1690–1710. *Museum of the City of New York*

(above)
Dressing table (lowboy)
William and Mary, New England, walnut, 1700–1720. *Wadsworth Atheneum*

(right)
High chest (highboy)
William and Mary, New York, gumwood, c. 1690. *The Metropolitan Museum of Art*

the figures were raised through the use of layers of gesso. Boston was the chief area where the art of japanning flourished.

A regional form of case furniture which developed in areas influenced by Dutch settlement (New York and New Jersey) was the *kas* shown below. These large wardrobes rest on bun feet, have a heavy cornice and doors on the front with shelves inside. They are based on the Dutch *kast* form which was often elaborately inlaid. In America, the *kas* was generally plain, although a few examples do exist with elaborate *grisaille* paintings of swags of fruit and flowers and sometimes trumpeting angels. That these pieces were a particularly popular form is testified to by the fact that the Egerton family of cabinetmakers in Northern New Jersey continued to make them into the late years of the 18th century.

(bottom left)
High chest (highboy)
Queen Anne, Boston, maple and pine with japanned decoration, c. 1735. *The Metropolitan Museum of Art*

(bottom right)
Kas
William and Mary, New York, pine with painted decoration, c. 1700. *Sleepy Hollow Restorations*

The table form represents a further refinement of types which had begun to develop in the last quarter of the 17th century. The turnings on gate-leg tables became more delicate and the movable members more complicated. The butterfly table with outward splaying legs became a particularly popular form, see page 3. The positioning of the legs, so that movement was outward from the centre, caused a greater delicacy to be introduced, and the use of butterfly supports enriched the form of such a piece. This table is apparently an American innovation as no prototypes have been found in Europe.

Seat furniture began to reflect the greater luxury and comfort of the period. The high-back armchair developed, which had upholstery on the back, sides, seat and arms as shown on page 27. It was a further evolution of the Cromwellian or Farthingale chair which had an upholstered back and seat with an open space between them. The high-back William and Mary armchair was the earliest form of the wing chair which was to enjoy great popularity during both the Queen Anne and Chippendale eras. These chairs often

(top)
Detail of mixing table
The top was made in Switzerland with slate in the center surrounded by marquetry panels

(above)
Mixing table
William and Mary, New England, walnut with slate and marquetry top, 1690–1710. *The Metropolitan Museum of Art*

(right)
Gate-leg table
William and Mary, New York, mahogany, c. 1700. *Albany Institute of History and Art*

(far right)
Arm chair (Boston chair)
William and Mary, New England, maple, with leather upholstery, 1700–1725. *The Henry F. duPont Winterthur Museum*

have baroque curves combined in the cresting and, at their best, have Spanish feet. Another type of chair combined caned panels in the seat and back, carefully imitating English prototypes. From this type of chair the day bed developed see page 26; it had a caned back and elongated seat. The back generally worked on a device so that it could be raised or lowered. These sometimes have elaborately carved crestings, flat vase-shaped balusters, curving arms, rush seats and turned legs, sometimes with Spanish feet. They were generally made of a number of different woods and were ebonized to disguise this. Chairs of this type were made in the areas of the Delaware and Hudson rivers. Another type incorporated a bent back, which had a center panel upholstered in leather. The seat was covered in the same material and the base had turned front legs with stretcher and flaring rear legs. This form, produced during the entire 18th century, is usually called the Boston chair.

It is unfortunate that such scant documentary material exists concerning makers of American William and Mary furniture. The name of Edward

Secretary
William and Mary, Philadelphia, Pennsylvania, walnut with cedar and pine, c. 1707. *Colonial Williamsburg*

Day bed
William and Mary, New Hampshire, early 18th century, *New Hampshire Historical Society*

Evans has been mentioned, but little is known of him except that he worked in Pennsylvania. More is known of the Gaines family of cabinetmakers because of examples of their work with documentation, as well as the existence of an important account book which is preserved at the Winterthur Museum. John Gaines (1677-c. 1750) was a turner of Ipswich, Massachusetts. His son, John (1704–1743) moved to Portsmouth, New Hampshire where he established a furniture shop. His work is chiefly known from a group of chairs which descended in his family. These chairs have a curved cresting piece, shaped back, vigorous arms, rush seat, and turned front legs terminating in Spanish feet. In other words they are similar to other chairs of the period, with one exception: Gaines used a single flat vase-shaped splat; this is actually a Queen Anne characteristic, so his work might be regarded as transitional of the two periods.

In general, it might be said that the first quarter of the 18th century in America saw the introduction of greater style and comfort to house interiors. The first academic interior architectural paneling was introduced at this time. Rooms were enriched with imported luxuries from Europe and the Orient. Elaborate frames for looking glasses were made, sometimes painted to simulate the popular tortoiseshell frames of Europe. Native furniture was beginning to show the simplicity of detail and flat plane surface which was to give it a different character from that of its European prototypes.

Arm chair
Late William and Mary, New
England, upholstered over maple
frame, c. 1700. *The Metropolitan
Museum of Art*

The Queen Anne style
1725–1755

Mixing table
Queen Anne, New York, mahogany
and marble, 1735–1745. *The Henry
F. duPont Winterthur Museum*

Side table
Chippendale, Massachusetts,
mahogany and marble, 1760–1775.
*The Henry F. duPont Winterthur
Museum*

By 1720, changes in the style of American furniture
had begun to take place. The change was slow and
transitional forms between the William and Mary
and Queen Anne styles developed; the new style was
not firmly established until c. 1730. In addition, the
elements of style associated with the Queen Anne
persisted throughout the remainder of the century,
although they became less popular by the middle of
the century.

The fundamental stylistic change came through the
use of the delicate curved cabriole leg. This scroll-like
element was first introduced into French decorative
art c. 1700. It led to the development of the rococo
(rockwork) style which was characterized by the use
of elaborate interlocking curves. In England, the
cabriole leg was first introduced during the reign of
Queen Anne (1702–1714) and was to continue in
popularity until c. 1760. The full rococo style did not
become popular in England until the middle of the
century. This occurred because pieces of furniture of
strong architectural form were still highly popular.
Attention was lavished on a scholarly interpretation
of proper proportion, pediments and moldings. This
popularity went hand-in-hand with neo-Palladian
building. Thus, the style popular in England might be
termed retarded rococo. American furniture called
Queen Anne also embraces the styles known in
England as George I and II.

English Queen Anne chairs generally followed two
forms. One was an interpretation of the Chinese chair
with a cresting which was almost flat with rounded
forms at each end and stiles were straight. The other
type had stiles of cabriole shape with an ornament
carved in the center of the hoop-shaped cresting. Each
of these forms had vase-shaped splats. Pad and hoof
feet were used first on these chairs but the ball-and-
claw foot was soon to become most popular. This foot
is thought to have originated in the Chinese dragon
claw with pearl.

The introduction of this style in the colonies came at
a time when strong regional characteristics were

28

developing in the use of materials. For instance, walnut, cherry, and maple were associated with New England furniture while walnut and imported mahogany came to be associated with New York and Philadelphia. Carving became more important than inlay for ornamentation. Inlay was restricted to star and sunburst patterns and triple bands of striping on

Gaming table
Chippendale, New York, mahogany, 1765–1780. *The Henry F. duPont Winterthur Museum*

drawer fronts. Finials, carved as urns or corkscrews, were used on pediments. Veneering was used on drawer fronts and chair splats. Japanning continued to be popular particularly in the Boston area, but it was done also in New York and, in a limited way, in Connecticut.

The Queen Anne period did not see the introduction of as many new furniture forms as the William and Mary. Many of the earlier forms were modified

Breakfast table
Queen Anne, Massachusetts,
white walnut, 1725–1745.
*The Henry F. duPont Winterthur
Museum*

Tea table
Queen Anne, Massachusetts,
walnut, 1720–1740. *The Henry F.
duPont Winterthur Museum*

(opposite)
Bed
Queen Anne, Rhode Island, maple,
with crewel hangings, 1735-1750.
*The Henry F. duPont Winterthur
Museum*

in the new style. The introduction of the fashion of tea drinking in the 1730s caused certain new forms to be created. The dish-top tea table with cabriole legs and the rectangular-top tea table became important. The tea table with tripod base appeared. Sometimes this had a birdcage attachment under the top which makes it possible to tilt and turn the top. This type became especially popular during the Chippendale years; it was a piece which was highly movable and took up little space when not in use.

The card table with folding top and round corners was introduced to the colonies at this time. The high chest or highboy developed as a peculiar American form which was to persist through most of the remainder of the century. It was characterized by a broken-arch pediment and large shells carved on the top center drawer and the bottom drawers. The secretary-bookcase generally followed the same form in its pediment. This characteristic does not duplicate anything English and seems to be an original development of American furniture. One theory which has been advanced is that the broken arch was borrowed from English-looking glasses with architectural pediments which were being imported into the colonies by the beginning of the second quarter of the century.

The day bed, similar in form to its William and Mary prototype, remained popular. The splat of the adjustable back was now vase-shaped and the piece often was supported on cabriole legs. The slope-front desk remained a popular form because of the usefulness of the drawers incorporated into it. Some remarkably beautiful desks-on-frames also were made. The upholstered setee now began to appear. Early examples show the influence of high-back chairs, but, by the middle of the century, a form had developed with a straight low back which was longer. Generally the term 'settee' is used for a short piece and 'sofa' for a piece on which one can recline. The upholstered easy chair (wing chair) continued in great popularity.

A dining table developed of gate-leg type. It was of the drop-leaf variety with the leaves supported by a single cabriole leg which was attached to a swinging gate. The bed with tester (frame-work for holding curtains) became popular, see opposite. Low beds, more characteristic of the 17th century, continued to be made, but the tester bed became popular in more fashionable houses. Sometimes the tester was arched

High chest (highboy)
Queen Anne, Connecticut, cherry wood painted, c. 1730–1740. *The American Museum in Britain, Bath*

so that it might fit under the low ceiling of an attic room. The field bed was also a development of this period. The name probably originated with beds which could be disassembled easily and were used in military campaigns. Looking glasses and clock cases began to be produced in the colonies and these closely followed English forms.

It has been mentioned that regional woods came to typify certain areas of American cabinetmaking. Regional characteristics became so pronounced by the Queen Anne period that in some instances it is possible to distinguish a piece made in one locale from that made in some other. This development was much more pronounced in the colonies than in any part of England. It probably occurred because the small groups of craftsmen settled in areas of different geography, climate, and raw materials. This, plus the fact that communication among the colonies took time and travel was slow, caused a certain isolation. Whatever the reason, might have been, it is remarkable that these early craftsmen were able to produce such beautiful and original statements of English style.

Some of the chief regional characteristics of American Queen Anne furniture, are treated here, going from north to south through the chief centers of cabinetmaking. Massachusetts furniture tended to be conservative and characteristics of the William and Mary period, such as stretchers connecting the legs of chairs, tended to disappear more slowly. The furniture of this area is generally delicate and spare; it has a verticality unlike that found in any other area. Highboys are slender, vertical and rise on delicate cabriole legs. Side chairs have a kind of pinched back and the vase-shaped splat is noted for its simplicity. Pieces which particularly show the Massachusetts style to its best advantage are the tea table and card table.

Newport, Rhode Island developed a style which was more original than that of any other American center, see page 48. This port first became a cabinetmaking center during the Queen Anne period but it did not witness a complete flowering of the craft until after the middle of the century. The Goddard and Townsend families of cabinetmakers are chiefly associated with this area. Santo Domingo mahogany was almost exclusively used. The ball-and-claw foot was adopted quite early here and is characterized by its oval shape rather than round. The talons are slender and outstretched and sometimes the ball-and-claw

form is pierced. This is reminiscent of English work and is generally associated with the cabinetmaker John Goddard. Splats on Newport chairs are generally narrow and often scrolled; the shell carved on the cresting is silhouetted, a characteristic also found on New York chairs. A flat serpentine stretcher is also to be found on some Newport chairs. It is, however, in the field of case furniture and the development of the block front that Newport is chiefly remembered today. This development, which reached its height after the mid-century, will be discussed under the Chippendale style.

The period of Dutch settlement in the colony later known as New York was relatively brief. However, certain characteristics of Dutch baroque design persisted in the furniture made there during much of the 18th century, see page 37. New York furniture has a square, squat, heavy feeling. The chair back is often nearly square and the cabriole legs have a sturdiness not to be found in any other area. The

Easy chair
Queen Anne, Rhode Island, walnut, 1735–1745. *The Henry F. duPont Winterthur Museum*

Block front dressing table (lowboy)
Queen Anne, Massachusetts, walnut, 1740–1750. *The Henry F. duPont Winterthur Museum*

33

ball-and-claw foot has a square quality and the rear leg, which is tapered and rounded, ends in a small square foot. A scroll, called a cupid's bow, is often found at the base of the splat in these chairs. Rich, crisp gadrooning is used on seat rails and tables. The New York card table, with deep gadrooning, is one of the most satisfactory and original forms developed in this center.

The most spectacular Queen Anne chairs were produced in Philadelphia, see page 36. The cresting is fashioned like a hoop and carved with S-shape spirals and, if a shell is included, it is contained in the design and not silhouetted. The splat has curved volutes and scrolls and the seat is horse-shoe shaped. The trifid foot is only seen on Philadelphia chairs and it is often paneled. Paneling similar to this is seen with

(below)
Common room, Ferry House, Van Cortlandt Manor
Queen Anne/Chippendale, Croton-on-Hudson, New York, mid 18th century. *Sleepy Hollow Restorations*

(opposite above)
Crewel bed hangings
Indian influence, made by Mary Bullman, 1745. *The Old Gaol Museum, York, Maine*

(opposite below)
Room from Hart House
Ipswich, Massachusetts, c. 1640. The earliest type of New England room. *The Metropolitan Museum of Art*

(below)
Arm chair
Chippendale, New York, walnut,
1730–1750. *The Henry F. duPont
Winterthur Museum*

the club and slipper foot; this would seem to have its origins in Irish cabinetmaking. The rear leg on Philadelphia chairs is often of the stump type; it is severely plain and round, although sometimes chamfered.

Furniture made in both New Jersey and Maryland bears a strong relation to the Philadelphia school, see page 40. Virginia furniture displays a kind of provinciality which links it with English country prototypes. Walnut and some fruitwood were the principal materials during the Queen Anne period, with southern yellow pine for secondary purposes. Tables have straight, rounded legs ending in slanting pad feet while case pieces have simple bracket feet. Charleston, South Carolina flourished as a cabinetmaking center during the Chippendale era. It is interesting to note that most documented southern furniture does not have the height or architectural proportion associated with centers to the north. The highboy form is not associated with the furniture of either Virginia or the Carolinas.

Some information is available about cabinetmakers working in the Queen Anne style, as they sometimes labeled or signed their pieces. John Gaines (died 1743) of Portsmouth, New Hampshire previously was mentioned in connection with the William and Mary style. He continued as an active cabinetmaker until his death but no furniture by him solely in the Queen Anne style has yet been identified. Robert Crossman (active *c.* 1730–1799) of Taunton, Massachusetts is also chiefly associated with the William and Mary style. He has been identified as the maker of the so-called Taunton chest. These chests are characterized by a painted decoration of vines and scrolls with birds sometimes included. An important chest attributed to Crossman is dated 1729 and can be seen in the collection at Historical Hall, Taunton.

(bottom left)
Arm chair
Queen Anne, New England, walnut, 1740–1760. *The Henry F. duPont Winterthur Museum*

(bottom right)
Easy chair
Chippendale, Philadelphia, mahogany, 1780–1790. *The Henry F. duPont Winterthur Museum*

Thomas Johnston (or Johnson) was active in Boston between 1732 and 1767 as an engraver and japanner. A trade card engraved for Johnston was decorated with cherubs' heads and this motif is to be seen on japanned furniture of superior quality, such as the matching highboy and lowboy in the American Wing at The Metropolitan Museum of Art. A superb highboy in the Winterthur Museum made by John Pimm of Boston, is thought to have been decorated by Johnson, see opposite. The Goddard-Townsend families of cabinetmakers of Newport, Rhode Island early began to work in the Queen Anne style. A labeled secretary by Job Townsend (1699–1765) made about 1730–1750 is preserved in the museum of the Rhode Island School of Design. This displays all the popular architectonic characteristics of case furniture of the time. It was Job Townsend and his son-in-law John Goddard (1723–1785) who founded the line of cabinetmakers.

(above)
Parlor of the Nicholas Schenck house
Flatlands, Brooklyn, c. 1755. The persistence of 17th century forms into the 18th century is demonstrated in the furnishing of this room. *The Brooklyn Museum*

(opposite)
High chest of drawers
Boston, maple and pine, 1740–1750. This japanned piece in the Queen Anne style was made by John Pimm for Commodore Joshua Loring and probably lacquered and painted by Thomas Johnson. *The Henry F. duPont Winterthur Museum*

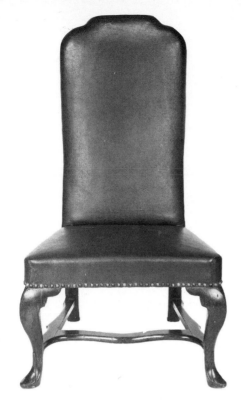

Side chair
(with upholstered back), Queen Anne, Pennsylvania, walnut, 1730–1740. *The Henry F. duPont Winterthur Museum*

Side chair
Chippendale, Philadelphia or New Jersey, mahogany, 1755–1765. *The American Museum in Britain, Bath*

William Savery (active 1740–1787) of Philadelphia is probably the best known American maker associated with the Queen Anne style, see opposite. The discovery of Savery's label in the drawer of a lowboy caused most fine Philadelphia furniture to be attributed to him for many years. Savery was a Quaker, so his furniture has a simplicity of ornamentation combined with a thorough knowledge of current design. Most of his labeled work is in the Chippendale style, but some interesting pieces, such as the labeled armchair at Winterthur, show the transition from the Queen Anne into this style. Thomas Elfe (active before 1747) of Charleston, South Carolina is another maker whose chief attributed works fall in the later period.

It should be remembered that traffic between the colonies, by land and sea, was steadily increasing as the century advanced. Therefore, it was possible for craftsmen to see furniture which was being made in the other colonies. In 1732, Daniel Henchman of Boston published the first American road guide, which he called *The Vade Mecum of America: Or a Companion for Traders and Travellers*. This work listed roads and taverns from Maine to Virginia and even included the dates when important fairs were held. By 1728 a regular packet service was established between New York and Charleston to facilitate trade, and furniture was among the trade items.

A boom in the building of houses—especially country houses of prestigious size—also, characterized the period. It was during the 1720s that Thomas Lee built his great house Stratford on the banks of the Potomac River in Virginia. Another house, Stenton, was built at the same time in the outskirts of Philadelphia, by James Logan, the former secretary to William Penn. Such houses echoed the interest in architecture and architectural design which was popular in England. Architectural design books became an important part of the library of the colonial. Hardly a house was built in the colonies which did not owe some debt to these design manuals.

Few of the existing houses from the period contain a complete Queen Anne interior. One of the most complete is the parlor from Readbourne, a house built in Queen Anne's County, Maryland, in 1733; it is now installed at the Winterthur Museum, see page 42.

The chimneybreast is set across the corner of the room and the fireplace opening is surrounded by Dutch tiles and a bolection molding. The walls are

Side chair
Queen Anne/Chippendale,
Philadelphia, walnut, 1740–1750.
*The Henry F. duPont Winterthur
Museum*

Corner chair
Chippendale, Newport, walnut,
1735–1750. *The Henry F. duPont
Winterthur Museum*

Side chair
Queen Anne, similar to labeled
examples by William Savery,
Philadelphia, curly maple, 1745–
1755. *The Henry F. duPont
Winterthur Museum*

completely paneled above and below a dado, with
fielded panels rising to a molded cornice. The room is
furnished with pieces in the Queen Anne style which
well typify the sophistication and grace with which
the colonial cabinetmaker could interpret the style.

(above)
The Readbourne parlor
Queen Anne County, Maryland,
1733. The best of the American
design is to be seen here. *The
Henry F. duPont Winterthur
Museum*

(opposite)
Deming parlor
Colchester, Connecticut, c. 1788.
Pieces from several cabinetmaking
centers are shown here: the
secretary-bookcase is from
Connecticut and the side chair to
its right from New York (Van
Rensselaer type). *The American
Museum in Britain*

The Chippendale style 1755–1785

The late 1750s saw the introduction to America of an Anglo-French rococo furniture style. This style flourished in the sixties and seventies and began to lose favor in the 1780s. Basic Queen Anne forms which were dominated by the cabriole leg continued to be used. Mahogany chiefly was employed in cabinetmaking and the ball-and-claw foot was highly popular; rich ornamental carving was popular in preference to veneer and inlay. This style had its origins in England in the 1730s and 1740s. Three forces combined to create it: the French rococo style; Chinese ornament which was known from imported objects; and the Gothic style, which had always remained a part of English tradition. These often were incorporated into pieces of furniture which retained

High chest (highboy)
Chippendale, Philadelphia, mahogany, 1760–1775, *Museum of Fine Arts, Boston*

the Palladian architectural influence so admired during the Queen Anne period. Thus the broken-arch pediment, pilaster and use of classic entablature of architrave, frieze, and cornice remained an essential part of furniture design.

The rococo style had found wide acceptance in England in the 1740s. It had originated in France in the 1720s with the introduction of curvilinear lines and lighter forms. While certain designers of the Louis XIV period introduced elements which were to form its background, the style was brought to fruition by such men as Juste-Aurèle Meissonier (c. 1693–1750) Gilles-Marie Oppenord (1672–1742), and Jean Pillement (1728–1801). The name, taken from *rocaille* refers to tock work or rock forms. These, along with *coquilles* (shell-patterns) appeared in an infinite variety of forms and combinations. Chinese patterns were further combined with naturalistic plant and animal forms to create an element of fantasy in the style. Asymetry was introduced through the cartouche ornamental tablet which was elaborately developed in many ways. It was the fanciful and fantastic combination of these elements that gave originality to the style.

Early among published English furniture designs which showed rococo influence were some crude plates in Batty and Thomas Langley's *City and Country Builders and Workman's Treasury of Designs* (1740). In the same year a work appeared which can be credited with popularizing the style in England: it was *A New Drawing Book of Ornaments* by Matthias Lock. This book contained elaborate designs, in cartouche form, for looking glasses and wall lights. It is interesting to note that in this and other works including, M. Lock's and H. Copland's *A New Book of Ornaments* (1752), rococo elements were applied to the earlier, basically square English forms. Even the cabriole leg never lost its strong verticality, in opposition to French forms.

Chinese influence has two chief components: the adaptation of actual Eastern furniture details, and *chinoiserie*, which was the Western imaginative interpretation of Chinese design. The first Chinese lattice designs published in England were in William Halfpenny's *New Designs for Chinese Temples* (1750). Highly influential was Edwards' and Darly's *New Book of Chinese Designs* (1754) published the same year as Chippendale's *Director*, which will be discussed below. A more scholarly and precise view of Chinese design was seen in William Chambers' *Designs of Chinese Buildings, Furniture, Dresses, Machines and Utensils*, published in 1757. Chambers had actually visited China and had made drawings there, so his work did not have the pseudo-Chinese feeling of some of his predecessors.

The final influence in the creation of the Chippendale style was the introduction of Gothic detail. As previously stated, it had never completely disappeared from the vocabulary of English design, as it was used in church and public architecture. Batty *Langley's Gothic Architecture Improved* (1742) showed buildings in the pseudo-Gothic style, and Horace Walpole purchased Strawberry Hill in 1747, and spent years remodeling it in the Gothic taste. He even designed furniture for it which incorporated elements from Gothic architectural design. In plates dated 1750 and 1751 in Darly's *New Book of Chinese, Gothic, and Modern Chairs*, the Gothic influence is first seen in English furniture design. It should be remembered that this furniture bore little or no resemblance to medieval English furniture and that Gothic elements were often so synthesized with rococo and Chinese forms that it is difficult to distinguish them.

It was Thomas Chippendale (1718–1779) who was to codify the style and to give his name to it in both England and America. He was born in Otley, Yorkshire to a father who was a joiner. Chippendale was in London by 1748 and in 1753 moved to St. Martin's Lane, where he was to remain throughout his life. He was succeeded by his son Thomas and his partner, Thomas Haig. His accounts show that he worked for a number of important families of the time, and his most famous work was executed for Nostell Priory and Harewood House, for which records exist, as well as some of the furniture. Chippendale is remembered chiefly, however, for his publication *The Gentleman and Cabinet-Makers Director*, which first appeared in 1754. It contained 160 engraved plates along with several describing the five orders of classic architecture. In 1755 a second edition which was unchanged was published; in a third edition (1762) some plates were omitted and over 100 new ones were added. This was the first English book to illustrate furniture of all straight square leg and lattice motif show the influence of Chinese design and the Gothic fret and arch were sometimes used. The rococo influence was chiefly

High chest (highboy)
Chippendale, Philadelphia, the Gratz highboy, mahogany, 1769 (documented date). *The Henry F. duPont Winterthur Museum*

kinds and its influence was felt over much of Europe as well as in America.

The *Director*, which was dedicated to the Earl of Northumberland, includes a list of subscribers which offers an interesting commentary on taste of the day. Twenty members of the nobility were subscribers, along with 90 cabinetmakers, 20 upholsterers, 10 carvers, nine joiners, and four carpenters as well as plasterers and makers of picture frames. Chippendale also worked in the later classical style. The famous pieces made for Harewood House between 1766 and 1770 were in this style and not in the rococo which had been popularized by the *Director*. It is not possible to determine exactly when Chippendale's name came to be identified with this type of furniture, but it surely was not earlier than the late 19th century.

The influence of the *Director* was felt in a number of America's cabinetmaking centers when the book was imported. However, the colonial pieces often displayed the survival of Queen Anne details and generally did not combine the rococo, Chinese and Gothic designs as elaborately as English models. The

Hall from Rensselaerswyck
Albany, New York, 1765–1768. Masterpieces of Chippendale furniture are shown in this hall set against English wallpaper. *The Metropolitan Museum of Art*

Desk
Chippendale, New York, mahogany, 1765–1780. *The Henry F. du Pont Winterthur Museum*

Dining room, Manor House, Van Cortlandt Manor
Croton-on-Hudson, New York, 18th century. Chippendale style chairs surround an early William and Mary gateleg table. *Sleepy Hollow Restorations*

felt in the use of C or S scrolls, in varied combinations, and in the elaborate treatment of the cartouche form which so characterized high-style Philadelphia furniture. Naturalistic surface carving often introduced characteristic rococo asymetry.

Some furniture forms persisted with little change, other than ornamentation, from the Queen Anne period. Chief among these were pieces of case furniture. The slant-front desk, secretary bookcase, and chest-on-chest were very popular among these forms. Chests of drawers were made in great quantities; these could be of a single rectilinear shape or they could have serpentine or reverse serpentine front, see page 55. Sometimes the chest had a top drawer especially fitted for cosmetics and toiletries, thus converting it to a dressing chest. The drop-leaf table retained its essential Queen Anne form, which was modified only through the introduction of ball-and-claw feet. This change was also to be observed in the side or mixing table which continued to be popular for dining room use. The highboy and lowboy persisted in fashion from the Queen Anne period when they had developed as relatively unique American forms. Shell motifs were introduced on the fronts of pieces made in Philadelphia and Newport and the cartouche was

(above)
Block-front secretary bookcase
Chippendale, Kingston or Newport, associated with the Goddard and Townsend families, mahogany, 1770–1780. *The Henry F. duPont Winterthur Museum*

(right)
Desk on frame
Queen Anne, New England, walnut, inlaid, 1735–1750. *The Henry F. duPont Winterthur Museum*

(above)
Wardrobe
Chippendale, New York, mahogany,
c. 1775–1790. *Sleepy Hollow
Restorations*

(left)
Block-front secretary bookcase
Chippendale, Massachusetts,
mahogany, 1765–1775. *The Henry
F. duPont Winterthur Museum*

49

Chest on chest
Chippendale, Philadelphia,
mahogany, 1760–1775. *Philadelphia
Museum of Art*

Block-front chest on chest
Chippendale, Newport, typical of
the work of Goddard and
Townsend families, mahogany,
1765–1780. *The Henry F. duPont
Winterthur Museum*

used as a finial on imposing Philadelphia case pieces.

During the period, a far greater luxury developed in interiors and a number of new and specialised furniture forms were created. The sofa had developed gradually from the Queen Anne settee. The Chippendale sofa often had a serpentine back and incorporated cabriole legs with ball-and-claw feet or straight square legs ending in a block (Marlborough), see below. The Pembroke table, with a large center top and short drop leaves, developed and was popular as a breakfast table. A new form rare in American furniture was the

Sofa
Chippendale, Newport, made by Adam S. Coe, mahogany, 1812. *The Henry F. duPont Winterthur Museum*

High chest (highboy)
Chippendale, Philadelphia, mahogany, 1765–1775. *Houston Museum of Fine Arts*

Sofa
Chippendale, Philadelphia, mahogany, 1765–1780. *The Henry F. duPont Winterthur Museum*

breakfront. This consisted of a bookcase with drawers and a closed section below. Sometimes the closed section projected beyond the top, thus giving the piece its name.

The fashion for tea drinking was responsible for the further introduction of new forms. The kettle stand was a small, easily movable piece which often was created with great elaboration, see page 54. The fret top 'china table' was used to hold all the paraphernalia necessary for the proper service of tea see opposite. An elaborate 'piecrust' top developed at this time for the tripod, tilt top tea table. Specialized pieces were also developed for holding candles (candlestands), see page 54, and the basin stand reflected a sophistication

Dining table
Chippendale, New York, 1755–1765. *The Henry F. duPont Winterthur Museum*

Side table
Chippendale, New York, mahogany and marble, 1760–1775. *The Henry F. duPont Winterthur Museum*

China table
Chippendale, New York, mahogany,
1765–1775. *The Henry F. duPont
Winterthur Museum*

Breakfast table
Queen Anne, New England, walnut,
painted, 1720–1740. *The Henry F.
duPont Winterthur Museum*

Tea table
Queen Anne, New England, maple
painted, 1720–1740. *The Henry F.
duPont Winterthur Museum*

Tea table
Chippendale, Newport, made by
John Goddard, mahogany, 1763
(documented date). *The Henry F.
duPont Winterthur Museum*

of style. The blockfront chest of drawers is associated with this period, as is the kneehole desk or dressing table. The blockfront chest is chiefly identified with New England, although some examples were made in New York.

Looking glasses became far more elaborate and often reflected the rich resources of Chippendale design, see page 56. Many of the American shops

Kettle stand
Chippendale, Newport, probably by John Townsend, mahogany, 1770–1785. *The Henry F. duPont Winterthur Museum*

Candlestand
Chippendale, Newport, associated with Goddard and Townsend families, mahogany, 1760–1780. *The Henry F. duPont Winterthur Museum*

Tea table
Chippendale, Philadelphia, mahogany, 1765–1775. *The Henry F. duPont Winterthur Museum*

Fire screen
Chippendale, New York, mahogany, 1760–1775. *The Henry F. duPont Winterthur Museum*

Chest of drawers
Chippendale, Philadelphia, made by Jonathan Gostelowe, mahogany, 1775–1780. *The Henry F. dupont Winterthur Museum*

(below, left to right)
Looking glass
Chippendale, Philadelphia, made by James and Henry Reynolds, mahogany and gilt, c. 1790. *The Henry F. duPont Winterthur Museum*

Looking glass
Chippendale, New York, pine with gilt and paint, c. 1765. *Sleepy Hollow Restorations*

Looking glass
Chippendale, Philadelphia, labeled by John Elliott, Sr, mahogany and gilt, 1753–1761. *The Henry F. duPont Winterthur Museum*

which made looking glasses also advertised that they imported from England. Therefore, because of the proximity of English models, it is often difficult to determine the place of origin of a looking glass except by an analysis of the materials of construction. Three distinct forms were made. The most oldfashioned was that with fret work at the top and bottom which was actually a slightly more elaborate development from the Queen Anne. The architectural type, with broken-arch pediment and entablature, was a standard form of the period. The most elegant was the rococo gilt looking glass, which carefully adhered to the cartouche form in its overall shape and ornamentation.

Regional characteristics remained important in the Chippendale period. As in the case of the Queen Anne style, Massachusetts furniture was slower to change

form than that of other schools. The slender and highly refined cabriole leg is typical of this area, with the block-and-spindle stretcher often retained for seat furniture. The ball-and-claw is crisply carved with the side talon turned back sharply, forming a triangle with the center claw when observed from the side. The same feeling of delicacy is to be found in tables from the area with tall, slender cabriole legs. A form of tea table which developed is the turreted or buttress top type. Here, circular projections extended from the top of the piece so that tea cups could be placed in them. Chests-on-chests and secretaries often had flattened pilasters framing the upper section. Corkscrew finials were popular and sometimes carved human figures were introduced for this use. The Skillin family of Boston is chiefly remembered for this latter type of carving. The most important members were Simeon Skillin, Sr (1716–1778) and his sons John (1746–1800) and Simeon, Jr (1757–1806). Their most famous extant work is the carving on the chest-on-chest made by Stephen Bodlan in 1793 for Elias Hasket Derby of Salem. It is in the

(below)
Arm chair
Chippendale, Massachusetts, possibly by Joseph Short of Newburyport, mahogany, 1790–1795. *The Henry F. duPont Winterthur Museum*

(right)
Corner chair
Queen Anne, New England, maple with stain, 1725–1740. *The Henry F. duPont Winterthur Museum*

Stool
Chippendale, New York, walnut,
1750–1760. *The Henry F. duPont
Winterthur Museum*

Bed
Chippendale, New England, black
birch and soft pine, 1770–1785.
*The Henry F. duPont Winterthur
Museum*

(opposite)
Bed
Chippendale, Massachusetts,
mahogany with hangings, 1760–
1775. *The Henry F. duPont
Winterthur Museum*

Yale University Art Gallery, where it is a part of the
Garvan Collection.

Block-fronts on case pieces are also characteristic of
Massachusetts. In general, however, they are somewhat flatter in feeling than those found on Newport
pieces. Benjamin Frothingham (1734–1809) is a
Boston area cabinetmaker who has been identified
with this type of blocking. Labeled or signed pieces
by this maker are known in the Queen Anne, Chippendale, and Federal styles. His particular treatment
combined blocking, or the contrast of raised against
recessed surfaces, with reverse serpentine construction.
The most ambitious form which is characteristic of
this school is the kettle or bombé base for case
pieces. This great bulging base had its origins in
rococo designs as it was a characteristic form in
French Louis XV case furniture. Only a highly
skilled cabinetmaker could create such a piece. John
Cogswell (active 1769, died 1818) is a Boston maker
closely identified with this form. Several examples
exist with signatures which show that he understood
the principles of rococo design both in the bombé
base and in his handling of surface ornamentation.
Joseph Hosmer (1735–1821), another maker of the
Massachusetts school from Concord, executed highly
original pieces in cherry.

In New Hampshire, a family of cabinetmakers named Dunlap worked in a curious and individual statement of the Queen Anne and Chippendale styles, see below. Their work is identified more with that of the country craftsman and it is later in date than the flourishing of the style in important cabinet-making centers. Because of the use of many Chippendale characteristics it is included here. The Dunlaps worked in Goffstown and Salisbury, chiefly in curly maple. Proportions of both chairs and case pieces have a distinct individuality. Case pieces generally rest on squat cabriole legs with pad feet. Galleries with carved basketwork are found on these pieces as well as S scrolls flatly carved in an elongated shape. Shells

(below left)
High chest (highboy)
Chippendale, New Hampshire, probably made by Samuel Dunlap II, maple, 1775–1790. *The Henry F. duPont Winterthur Museum*

(below right)
Chest on chest
Chippendale, New Hampshire, probably by a member of the Dunlap family, maple, 1768–1800. *The Currier Gallery of Art*

often have characteristic pinwheels when treated by these cabinetmakers. The account books of John and Samuel Dunlap have revealed much documentary material concerning their furniture. John (1746–1792) had an established cabinetshop in Goffstown. On March 5, 1773 Lieutenant Samuel (1752–1830) began working in his brother's shop. The latter eventually settled in Salisbury, where his account books cover the period 1780–1820. The earliest entries in John's account book date from 1768.

It will be remembered that certain members of the Goddard and Townsend families of Newport had begun their careers working in the Queen Anne style. The handling of the blockfront and shell by this school represents the most original type of American cabinetmaking prior to the Revolution, see page 48. Rich, highly figured Santo Domingo mahogany was the chief wood. Blocking was created by projecting sections contrasting with recessed sections. While this is generally carved from a single piece of wood, examples are found where the projecting areas are glued on. This treatment is rare in English furniture; it more frequently appears on Dutch case pieces and its extensive use in Newport has not satisfactorily been explained. Shells, which were sometimes applied, were carved in high relief and contain fine incised detail. A flattened finial, which has been termed 'cup-

Side chair
Queen Anne/Chippendale, Newport, walnut, 1740–1750. *The Henry F. duPont Winterthur Museum*

(right)
Breakfast table
Chippendale, Newport, made by John Townsend, mahogany, 1760–1780. *The Henry F. duPont Winterthur Museum*

cake', with corkscrew extending from it, often adorns case pieces. Ogee-bracket feet have a small scroll and the palmette is sometimes carved on knees. The ball-and-claw foot is oval in shape and the talons sometimes undercut.

Job Townsend (1699–1765) was a Quaker who established his shop on Easton's Point in Newport. It was his son-in-law John Goddard (1723–1785), along with John and Edmund Townsend, who brought the Newport Chippendale style to its highest state of development. In all, 23 members of these families supplied furniture through three generations and stylistically it ranges from the Queen Anne to the Empire style.

Dressing table (lowboy)
Queen Anne, Connecticut, cherry, 1740–1760. *The Henry F. duPont Winterthur Museum*

Connecticut produced an original type of furniture somewhat less sophisticated, see pages 64–65. Cherry, which was plentiful, was the chief wood employed. Elements of Queen Anne design, including the pad foot, were retained for a long time in this area. Connecticut furniture shows the influence of both the Newport and Philadelphia schools. Several cabinetmakers who worked in Connecticut came from Philadelphia but a documented source for the individual Connecticut block front and shell has not been determined. In general, a simpler treatment of the block front, a shallow version of the shell, and carved sunbursts or pin-wheel patterns characterize this furniture, see page 65. Lattice-work pediments

Bombé chest of drawers
Chippendale, Massachusetts, mahogany, 1765–1780. *The Henry F. duPont Winterthur Museum*

and scallops on the skirts of case pieces are more sophisticated design elements.

Members of the Chapin family are associated closely with this school. Eliphalet Chapin (1741–1807) was trained in Philadelphia and settled in East Windsor, Connecticut by 1771, and was active there until 1795. His work reflects the Philadelphia style through its elaborate lattice and scrolled pediments and a distinct type of finial characterized by a pierced four-

Block-front chest of drawers
Chippendale, Connecticut type made by Chapin family, cherry, 1770–1790. *The Henry F. duPont Winterthur Museum*

Dressing table (lowboy)
Chippendale, Philadelphia, mahogany, 1775–1780. *Sleepy Hollow Restorations*

sided cartouche. His second cousin Aaron Chapin (1753–1838) was apprenticed to him and worked with him until the latter's move to Hartford in 1783. Basic biographical and documentary evidence survives concerning Aaron, but it is virtually impossible to distinguish his work from that of his cousin. Benjamin Burnham (active 1769–1773) of Colchester, Connecticut is also identified with the school. There is an unusual block front desk by him in the American Wing at The Metropolitan Museum which bears his signature and the date 1769. This piece has a curious interior with 29 small drawers arranged in sloping tiers. The best single collection of Connecticut furniture is the Barbour Collection at The Wadsworth Atheneum in Hartford.

New York furniture was slow to change stylistically and rococo ornamentation made little headway, see page 68. The design vocabulary of George II furniture, with its strong reliance on architectural form, dominated the work of this city prior to the revolution. Characteristic of this earlier influence was the employment of the tassel and ruffle and strapwork enclosing a diamond in chair backs. Rare rococo influence came through the use of some Gothic motifs and the serpentine form employed in card

Chest on chest
Chippendale, Connecticut, made by
Reuben Beman, Jr, cherry, c. 1800.
*The Henry F. duPont Winterthur
Museum*

Arm chair
Chippendale, New York, mahogany,
1765–1775. *The Henry F. duPont
Winterthur Museum*

Side chair
Chippendale, Connecticut, New
Hampshire, maple, 1775–1790. *The
Henry F. duPont Winterthur
Museum*

tables. Both these and chairs often had skirts carved with gadrooning, which gives great elegance. In a sense, one can observe the persistence of the early Dutch baroque tradition in this furniture. It continued to be square, heavy and to have a kind of squat quality; these characteristics had persisted into the Queen Anne period and were carried forward to the Chippendale. Acanthus carving tended to be stringy. A distinctive ball and claw developed here. The foot has a square quality with the talons closely grasping it. The rear leg sharply tapers to a squared foot in the English manner. New York Chippendale furniture is chiefly known through tables and seat furniture, but several triangular pedimented secretaries have survived.

The Maple Room
Port Royal, Pennsylvania, 1762. Philadelphia-made furniture in maple is shown with paneling from an important Pennsylvania country house. *The Henry F. duPont Winterthur Museum*

The name of Gilbert Ash (1717–1785) has been associated with New York furniture and numerous pieces have been attributed to him, see page 68. He is listed in New York directories in 1748. He had a shop in Wall Street by 1756. The last known advertisement of his shop appeared in 1763, and chairs of mahogany and black walnut and mahogany tea and dining tables were mentioned. A small body of labeled and signed work by Ash exists. He frequently used a design of interlaced scrolls enclosing a diamond in chair backs, and cross-hatched lambrequins on the knee of cabriole legs. The deep gadrooning on the skirt also is to be seen in documented pieces by Thomas Burling, who was a Freeman in New York in 1769. He advertised from 1772–1775, left New York during the Revolu-

Dining room of the Francis Corbin house
Edenton, North Carolina, c. 1725. Palladian influence is seen in the triangular pediment above the fireplace. *The Brooklyn Museum*

Corner chair
Chippendale, New York, mahogany, 1760–1775. *The Henry F. duPont Winterthur Museum*

tion, but returned and was advertising again in 1785. He was joined in business by his son in 1791 and the last known advertisement of the shop dates from 1796. An important labeled wardrobe belongs to the New York Historical Society. Burling had been apprenticed to Samuel Prince (died 1778) who had been active in New York between 1772 and 1776. Gadrooning is characteristic of his work and his secretary-bookcases with triangular pediments have carved friezes.

It is certainly the mastery of the Philadelphia school which is most closely identified with the American Chippendale style, see pages 72–73. By the third quarter of the century, Philadelphia was the second largest English-speaking city in the world. In 1778, over 100 cabinetmakers and joiners and their journeymen marched in the parade celebrating the ratification of the Constitution. *The Rules of Work of the Carpenters' Company of the City and County of Philadelphia,* published in 1786, contains a remarkable series of plates which show the elaborate woodwork and chimney-breasts in the Palladian manner which were

being executed at the time. Cabinetmakers trained in European centers migrated to Philadelphia. Most of them came from London and Ireland, and Philadelphia furniture more than any other shows the influence of the distinct Irish school.

Philadelphia furniture more elaborately integrates and treats the rococo, Chinese and Gothic elements which make up the Chippendale style, than that of any other American center, see pages 71–73. The French scrolled toe, often shown in Chippendale's *Director*, was elaborated here. Surface carving, often illustrating the fables of Aesop, combined rococo and Chinese elements. The cartouche form was highly developed and often centered with a cabochon. The ball and claw achieved a sculpturesque quality with the talons finely articulated. The cabriole leg was often carved with acanthus in relief and in some rare instances terminated in a hairy paw foot; the only other center where the latter treatment is seen is in a few examples of Boston make. Furniture with straight square legs (Marlborough), was a favorite of Philadelphia, generally terminating in a block or plinth.

(below, left to right)
Side chair
Chippendale, New York, attributed to Gilbert Ash, mahogany, 1755–1765. *The Henry F. duPont Winterthur Museum*

Side chair (stuffed)
Chippendale, New York, mahogany, 1760–1775. *The Henry F. duPont Winterthur Museum*

Side chair
Chippendale, Philadelphia, mahogany, 1770–1780. *The Henry F. duPont Winterthur Museum*

Side chair
Chippendale, Philadelphia, mahogany, 1770–1780. *The Henry F. duPont Winterthur Museum*

(right)
Easy chair
Queen Anne, Philadelphia, walnut, 1735–1750. *The Henry F. du Pont Winterthur Museum*

(below)
The Kershner parlor
Wernersville, Pennsylvania, 1755. Pennsylvania German furniture shows some German and English influence. *The Henry F. duPont Winterthur Museum*

(opposite below)
Marriage chest
Pennsylvania, 1780–90. This white pine, painted chest suggests the work of the painter Johann Heinrich Otto. *The Henry F. duPont Winterthur Museum*

(opposite right)
Easy chair
Chippendale, Philadelphia, mahogany, 1760–1775. *The Henry F. du Pont Winterthur Museum*

(opposite left)
Easy chair
Chippendale, Philadelphia, mahogany, 1765–1775. *The Henry F. du Pont Winterthur Museum*

(below)
Bed (low post)
Chippendale, Philadelphia, walnut,
1750–1760. *The Henry F. duPont*
Winterthur Museum

(bottom)
Dressing table (lowboy)
Chippendale, Philadelphia, the
Gratz lowboy, mahogany, 1769
(documented date). *The Henry F.*
duPont Winterthur Museum

The work of William Savery (1721–1788) has been
mentioned previously in connection with the Queen
Anne style. He was a Quaker and chiefly catered to
this trade; his pieces in the Chippendale style are
relatively plain. An inventory of his shop indicates that
he did not own carving tools. He probably followed
the ordinary practice of constructing furniture and
employing others to carve it. Some 20 examples of
work bearing his label have come to light. Benjamin
Randolph (active c. 1760–1790) was the cabinetmaker who most elaborately employed elements of
the Chippendale style in Philadelphia cabinetmaking,
see page 74. He had established a cabinet shop in
Philadelphia about 1760. In 1770 he was using a trade
card engraved by J. Smither which incorporated
designs from Chippendale's *Director*. His receipt
books for 1763–1777 are in the collection of the

74

Winterthur Museum. He executed the now famous set of six 'sample' chairs, which rank among the highest efforts of 18th century colonial cabinetmaking. The wing chair of the group, at the Philadelphia Museum, is elaborately carved and has hairy paw feet. A side chair is also at Philadelphia and the four remaining side chairs are at the Winterthur Museum, Colonial Williamsburg, the Garvan Collection at Yale and in a private collection. Much simpler is the labeled side chair in the Karolik Collection at the Boston Museum.

The simpler chair by Randolph closely resembles a type made by James Gillingham (1736–1781), see page 76. This model has a trefoil pattern in the splat and is based on a design in Chippendale's *Director*, 1754 edition. Two of a set of these chairs are in the American Wing at the Metropolitan Museum. James had been apprenticed to his uncle John Gillingham

(opposite)
Side chair
Chippendale, Philadelphia, one of the 'sample' chairs attributed to Benjamin Randolph, mahogany, 1760–1775. *Philadelphia Museum of Art*

(below)
Catawba dining room
North-west Carolina, 1811. This extraordinary southern room shown Adamesque influence in the elaborate woodwork, sideboard and table. *Museum of Early Southern Decorative Arts*

Arm chair
Chippendale, Philadelphia, made by William Savery, walnut, 1755–1760. *The Henry F. duPont Winterthur Museum*

Side chair
Chippendale, Philadelphia, probably made by James Gillingham, mahogany, 1770–1780. *The Henry F. duPont Winterthur Museum*

(1710–1793). An inventory made at the time of his death would indicate that walnut was a favorite wood in his shop. Thomas Tufft (active before 1772, died 1788) took over the shops formerly occupied by James Gillingham in 1773. A pair of side chairs at Winterthur has an engraved paper label glued inside the back which reads 'Made and Sold by Thomas Tufft Cabinet and Chair Maker Four Doors from the Corner of Walnut Street in Second Street, Philadelphia.' The carving on his furniture is thought to have been executed by professionals after he had constructed the piece—the community of cabinetmakers working in Philadelphia was in close geographic proximity and some were related through marriage.

Daniel Trotter (1747–1800) produced a distinctive type of chair in his shop, see opposite. Today it is referred to as a 'pretzel-back' chair; essentially of the ladder-back type, the curved back slats cross one another leaving a round opening in the center, which resembles a pretzel. Trotter made chairs of this type for Stephen Girard of Philadelphia. He worked with his son-in-law Ephraim Haines (1775–1811). Bills have made possible the identification of Trotter and Haines' work from 1786 until about 1806. Thomas Affleck (1740–1795), was born in Scotland, probably received his training in England, and came to Philadelphia in 1763. He was one of the leading American exponents of the Chinese Chippendale style; this is reflected in the furniture he made for Governor John Penn's town house and for his country seat Lansdowne. Affleck is known to have owned a copy of Chippendale's *Director*. He was a Loyalist, was arrested in 1772 and banished to Virginia for seven months. He returned to Philadelphia, resumed work and continued to be patronized by the leading families of the city. He made furniture in 1794 for Congress Hall. John Elliott, Sr (1713–1791) was born in England and arrived in Philadelphia in 1753. Although he is known to have made furniture for the Shippen and Norris families, he is chiefly remembered through labeled looking glasses. As he was also an importer of these, the wood must be considered in determining a possible American origin.

John Folwell (active 1762, died 1780) was so much an admirer of Chippendale's work that he proposed the publication of his own American version of the *Director*. It was to be called *The Gentleman and Cabinet-Maker's Assistant Containing a Great Variety*

Arm chair
Chippendale, Philadelphia, type
made by Ephraim Haines and
Daniel Trotter, mahogany,
1770–1785. *The Henry F. duPont
Winterthur Museum*

Side chair
Chippendale, Baltimore, mahogany,
1765–1775. *The Henry F. duPont
Winterthur Museum*

of Useful and Ornamental Household Furniture, but was
never published. He followed a plate in the *Director*
when he designed the pediment for the case of the
orrery by David Rittenhouse, which is now in the
University of Pennsylvania. To him is also attributed
the speaker's chair made for the State House in 1779
and called John Hancock's Chair. Jonathan Shoe-
maker (active by 1757, died 1793) incorporated rococo
design into his furniture, which is chiefly distinguished
by the fineness and crispness of its carving.

Adam Hains (born 1768, working c. 1815) is
interesting because he continued to work in the
Chippendale style in Philadelphia after the Revolution. He is chiefly known for breakfast tables of the
Pembroke type. He moved to Berks county about
1803. The Backman family of cabinetmakers lived in
Lancaster County, Pennsylvania and produced furniture in the Chippendale style which had great individuality. There were five members of the family but it
is John II (1746–1829), who worked in the Chippendale style. It would appear that the Backmans were
principally custom cabinetmakers. Clock cases also
seem to be the first works of John II. He had been
trained in Switzerland and his work was influenced by
the Louis XV taste as well as that of contemporary
Philadelphia. During the Revolution, he apparently
made furniture for people in Lampeter Township
where he lived. Backman's furniture used Chippendale decorative details in such an original way that it is
often identifiable on a stylistic basis.

Considerable studies have been made in research
in the field of furniture made south of Philadelphia.
Southern furniture was often produced by itinerant
craftsmen, so that it is possible to develop certain
stylistic criteria, but often impossible to identify the
individual craftsman. The variety of walnut produced in the south (Juglans nigra) was generally pre-
ferred for furniture. It was only in Charleston that
mahogany was framed as early as the Queen Anne
period; walnut was sometimes used as a secondary
wood.

Furniture made in Maryland during the Chippendale years shows the strong influence of Philadelphia
taste. The development of Baltimore as an important
port came after the Revolution, so the school of
cabinet-making which flourished there was in the
Classical style. It was only in Charleston, South
Carolina, that a thriving school of cabinetmaking

survives from this period which is documented, but those examples reveal a sophisticated treatment which closely relates to English furniture. The chief Charleston cabinetmaker, about whom there is existing biographical material is Thomas Elfe, Sr (c. 1719–1775). It is thought that Elfe was born in London and served his apprenticeship there. He was advertising in Charleston as early as 1747, and in another advertisement of 1751 it was stated that Elfe had recently employed an upholsterer from London who was a specialist in drapery, curtains, and upholstery. He formed a partnership with Thomas Hutchinson as early as 1756, they were working together on balusters for the steeple of St. Michael's Church; they made a communion table for the church in 1763. Elfe's account books for the years 1768–1775 contain the names of his customers, prices paid for furniture and

Drawing room from the Samuel Powel house
Philadelphia, c. 1768. The richness of the fully developed rococo style is demonstrated in this room. *The Metropolitan Museum of Art*

a description of the individual pieces. The books are preserved in the Charleston Library Company. The eight years covered by the books reveal that about 1500 pieces were made in Elfe's shop. It also gives a clear picture of the large number of apprentices and slaves who worked there.

It is unfortunate that no examples of Elfe's work have come to light with a label or signature. However, the account books make it possible to trace the descent of some extant pieces and to attribute them positively to him. All pieces thus attributed are in the Chippendale style and are made of mahogany, with cypress as a secondary wood or they are of tulipwood. He made furniture which was elaborate as well as simple pieces. Favorite forms were tables, beds, chests-of-drawers, bookcases, secretary-bookcases, wardrobes, chairs and desks. The use of eagle claws for feet is a characteristic

The Sargent Family
by an unknown artist, oil, 1800. Shield-back side chairs and a Martha Washington chair are seen in this carefully depicted interior. *National Gallery of Art*

Arm chair
Chippendale, Maryland or
Pennsylvania, mahogany, 1755–
1770. *The Henry F. duPont
Winterthur Museum*

developed before the Revolution. Little furniture of his work; so too is an elaborate fret which he employed on case pieces and chimney pieces. Such detail necessitated an extra charge; an inventory of his possessions made at Elfe's death indicates that he was a wealthy man. He left his work benches and carpenter's tools to his son Thomas, Jr (1759–1825) but little is known of the latter's work.

All the furniture previously discussed has been conceived under a general English influence, with certain continental traditions such as Dutch and French playing a part. In the late 17th century, a group of settlers began to arrive from the German Rhineland and Switzerland. They brought with them a kind of peasant culture and tradition which was quite distinct from the other settlers. These groups, who were generally of dissident religious background, all settled in south eastern Pennsylvania in Bucks, Berks, Lancaster, Dauphin, Montgomery, and Lehigh Counties. Represented were Mennonites, Amish, Moravians, Dunkers and Lutherans. Those who settled in Pennsylvania popularly have been called 'Pennsylvania Dutch,' but Pennsylvania German is a more proper designation. Many Moravians moved south to Winston Salem, North Carolina, where they established a community.

The Pennsylvania-German cabinetmakers produced furniture which was in an earlier tradition, see opposite. Many of the motifs used on furniture have their origin in medieval illuminations. These were brightly painted on furniture, often with accompanying names and dates. Most of this type of furniture which is known today dates from the second half of the 18th century. Typical forms were dower chests; chairs with scrolled solid back, solid seat, and stick legs; dressers; cupboards; and wardrobes. The chief woods employed were walnut, oak, yellow pine and tulipwood. This furniture is resplendent with painted decorations of unicorns, tulips, hearts, horsemen, stars, vases, etc. and the painting is often of such a naïvely original character that it can be classified as a distinct type of American folk art, see page 71.

A Pennsylvania-German cabinetmaker about whom considerable is known is Christian Selzer (1749–1831). The name was undoubtedly originally spelled 'Seltzer.' Painted dower chests seem to have been his speciality and two survive which bear his signature in Gothic script and the dates 1771 and 1796.

No two of his chests were painted alike, and they vary slightly as to size and arrangement of the panels. After 1790 the panels became taller and the vases of flowers executed on them more delicate. The chests, generally made of soft white wood, are about 48 inches in length, and are left unfinished on the inside; three panels are the standard number and the chests are fitted with German-type hardware. There is a Selzer chest of this type in the American Wing at the Metropolitan Museum and one dated 1796 at the Philadelphia Museum.

(above)
Wardrobe (Schrank)
Pennsylvania German, inlaid
walnut, 1779 (dated). *Philadelphia
Museum of Art*

Tall case clock (left)
Chippendale, Pennsylvania,
Reading area, works by Asabel
Cheney, East Hartford, Connecticut,
walnut, 1801 (dated). *Yale
University Art Gallery*

Comb-back Windsor arm chair
Philadelphia, hickory, oak,
gumwood and maple, 1750–1780.
The Art Institute of Chicago

Windsor furniture was a type which carried on the joiner's tradition in the Chippendale era. This type was produced in quantity in England during the 17th century and apparently derived its name from the town of Windsor, which was an important market place. Stick construction typifies the Windsor chair, for it was made from stick legs and spindles driven into a plank seat, see opposite. They were being made in great numbers in Philadelphia in the early 1700s which caused them occasionally to be called 'Philadelphia' chairs. Hickory and ash were tough and springy and could be shaped, so they were ideal for Windsor construction, which required no screws or nails. The first Windsors made in Philadelphia had low backs; these were followed by comb-backs or bow-backs, and a New England version of continuous hoop-and-arm type. During the second half of the century, Windsors were being made in most major cities and were one of the most popular items of furniture, see page 75. Because these chairs and settees were made of a number of types of wood, they were painted such colors as red, black, blue, yellow, rose, gray or even painted with flowers. There are many variants on the Windsor type, such as cradles, high chairs, stools and writing-arm chairs. Windsors were exported from the colonies to many other parts of the world.

The Chippendale age was one in which there was a demand for the best in design and workmanship. Commercial prosperity caused a greater desire for luxury and comfort and new forms to satisfy them. Interior paneling became ever-increasingly elaborate. The hall from Rensselaerswyck (1765–1769), the great Van Rensselaer manor house near Albany, New York, or that from the Powel House in Philadelphia of 1768, both now installed in the American Wing, Metropolitan Museum, typify the grandeur which was enjoyed by some colonials, see pages 46, 78. Here, elaborate English wallpaper or stucco ceilings were combined with fine wood carving to create an effect meant to equal that of great English buildings of the time.

It is interesting to note that while Americans were listing their grievances against England, they were still under the influence of the architectural and design taste of their mother country. The Powel House was one of the grandest erected in Philadelphia. Patterns for the woodwork and stucco ceilings were largely

Tap room
Ferry House, Van Cortlandt Manor, Croton-on-Hudson, New York. A group of New York and New England Windsors is to be seen here. *Sleepy Hollow Restorations*

borrowed from Abraham Swan's *Designs in Architecture* (first London edition 1757). A comparison of the designs with the final execution shows that a vigor was injected which was original and yet faithful to the spirit of the plates.

The furniture created during this period fits into the same category. While it was strongly influenced by popular English design books, it cannot be considered as anything other than a local product. It was very rarely that any single design was copied. Through selection, rearrangement and often the addition of quite personal detail, a native style was created which had regional variations. More documentary evidence is available about this period than earlier times because of the practice of labeling and signing pieces. Pride in individual craftsmanship must have inspired this practice. Thus, it was during the Chippendale age that craftsmanship reached its height in colonial America.

Classical styles
1785–1850

Chest on chest
Chippendale/classical, Salem, made
by William Lemon with carving by
Samuel McIntire, mahogany, 1796.
Museum of Fine Arts, Boston

Shield-back side chair
classical, Massachusetts, mahogany,
1790–1800. *Yale University Art
Gallery*

The long time span cited in this chapter's title might cause wonderment in the minds of some readers. Actually, the entire continuum, in one way or another, reflects the design influence of classical Greece and Rome. Therefore, the material will be treated in this manner, rather than dividing it into different phases. Included here is material which has to do with the early phase (sometimes termed neo-classic or Adam-esque classicism), its successor, archaeological classicism (often called Empire), and finally the debased classical style of the 1840s and 1850s. It has been popular in recent years, to refer to the neo-classic and archaeological phase as the Federal Period and to give it the dates c. 1785–c. 1825.

From the opening years of the 18th century, European intellectuals and travelers were beginning to show a keen interest in classical antiquity. Discoveries at Herculaneum aroused a deep romantic interest in the past and caused numerous books to be published describing those and other antiquities.

The English architect William Kent (1685–1748) began to apply Greek keys and egg-and-dart moldings to what were otherwise Baroque forms as early as 1730. Designers in France and England followed Kent's example and such pieces were popular until the 1760s. Simultaneously, a new style began to appear. Robert Adam (1728–1792) was an English architect and designer who published an important work *Ruins of the Palace of the Emperor Diocletian* (1764). He had traveled extensively in Italy and had greatly admired Roman monuments such as the remains of houses unearthed at Pompeii and Hadrian's Villa, as well as the masterpieces of the Renaissance. Adam came to the conclusion that the application of classical details by Kent and others was too heavy. His belief that design should be light and delicate was to give an entirely new direction to English buildings and their interiors.

The style which Adam developed first appeared in the 1760s with the furniture which he designed in connection with the remodeling of Syon House and Osterley. (He has sometimes been credited with the development of the delicate straight leg, but there is considerable evidence to show that there was a similar development in France at the time.)

In this style, straight lines replaced the curved lines associated with the rococo. Furniture legs could be round or square and were delicately tapered. Pilasters

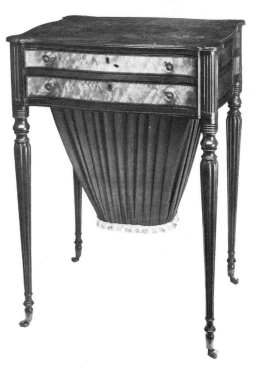

Serpentine work table
classical, Boston, possibly by John and/or Thomas Seymour, mahogany, 1800–1810. *The Henry F. duPont Winterthur Museum*

and moldings were used to emphasize structural lines. Popular devices were the patera, Greek key, guilloche, anthemion, husk festoons and cameo-like medallions. These were all handled in a light manner and delicacy is chiefly associated with the style. Favorite woods for pieces of furniture in this style were satinwood and harewood. Surfaces were decorated with veneered panels and inlays; painted figures and scenes were popular, while carving came to be used in a more limited way.

Two design books were responsible generally for the popularization of this style in furniture making. They were George Hepplewhite's *Cabinet-Maker and Upholsterer's Guide* (1788) and Thomas Sheraton's *Cabinet-Maker and Upholsterer's Drawing Book*. which was published in several editions between 1791 and 1794. The plates in the books of the two designers are often quite similar but some general statements can be made about the dominant taste in each. Hepplewhite was fond of the square tapering leg which often terminated in a spade foot. Inlay was favored and the chief decorative motifs were Prince-of-Wales feathers, medallions, drapery, and ears of what. A limited number of designs was also included in Hepplewhite's *Guide* which continued the tradition of the rococo through the use of curved lines. This was called the French style, and it bears a close resemblance to French forms. Sheraton favored the round, turned reeded leg in his book. These designs are more faithful to the spirit of the late Louis XVI style in France. Free-standing columns were incorporated into the corners of case pieces; these often ran the full height of the piece. Favorite chair backs were composed of bars, sometimes forming a kind of trellis effect.

The introduction of the classical style in America was gradual and transitional. The Chippendale style remained popular in the 1790s but it was often seen in combination with classical decorative motifs, see page 84. The flaring bracket foot was now to be seen on pieces with a broken-arch pediment and inlay was used on pieces in the earlier style. The chair back changed gradually until it achieved the shield back form which is associated with classicism.

After the Revolution, a new wave of cabinetmakers began to come to the United States from England, Ireland, Scotland and, in the early years of the 19th century, from France. They were familiar with popular European furniture design publications of the day and often brought copies of the books with them. They catered, in eastern centers, to a rising new class of wealthy merchants who were anxious to be abreast of fashion currents in Europe.

At this time the lowboy and highboy disappeared as furniture forms. The chest-on-chest continued in popularity and was often embellished with highly elaborate carving. The chest-on-chest in the Karolik collection at the Boston Museum, which was made in Salem in 1796 by William Lemon (active 1796) with carving by Samuel McIntire (1757–1811), is a superb example of this type, see page 84. While still retaining a Chippendale form, all the carving is executed in the classical taste.

Sideboard
classical, Salem, mahogany, c. 1800.
Museum of Fine Arts, Boston

The most important new form of the period was the sideboard, see pages 89, 105. It was a logical development from the side or mixing table. Drawers and compartments with doors were included and the entire piece was raised on legs. Sideboards were generally of two types: one had square legs with a recessed center section; the other had a kidney-shaped top which created round ends. In the South, the huntboard developed as a regional type. More closely identified with the side table, this piece usually had a high top on long legs and was quite long.

The work table was also a new form, see page 85. It was designed with the specific needs of the needleworker in mind. Work tables were fitted with sets of drawers with compartments or divisions. A cloth or (rarely) wooden 'bag' was included to hold the sewing. In the early years of the 19th century, such tables often became very complex in their arrangement and convertibility. Card tables were popular and

(below left)
Lady's writing desk
classical, Baltimore, mahogany and satinwood, c. 1800. *The Metropolitan Museum of Art*

(below right)
Dressing table
classical, Boston, variously attributed to Samuel McIntire and the Seymours, mahogany, satinwood and maple, c. 1795. *Essex Institute*

Desk
classical, Boston, attributed to
John and Thomas Seymour,
mahogany, holly and satinwood,
1795–1815. *Houston Museum of
Fine Arts*

they retained the swing-leg of their Chippendale predecessors. The top of the pembroke table was held in place by pulls; the leaves were rounded and, when extended, formed an oval. The sectional dining table became a well-known form in the classical period. It was sometimes in two sections with rounded ends and drop leaves so that it could be pushed together to form a single table. In other instances a third section with two drop leaves was added; this was used as the center of the table and the ends, when not in use, could be placed against the wall as side tables.

A dressing table evolved with an attached looking glass, see opposite. The glass was generally arranged so that it could be moved to suit the view of the person using it. The fall-front chest of drawers with a column at either end developed as a variation on the Chippendale chest. The slope-front desk was succeeded in popularity by the tambour desk at this time. The tambour was created from a number of strips of wood

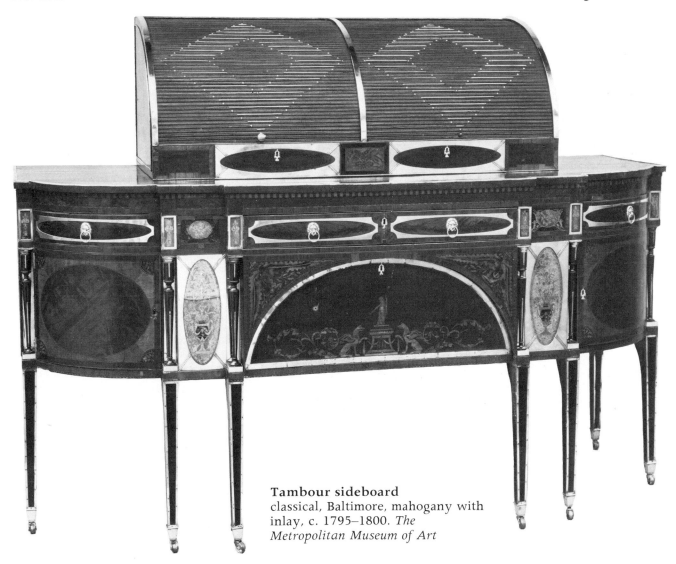

Tambour sideboard
classical, Baltimore, mahogany with
inlay, c. 1795–1800. *The
Metropolitan Museum of Art*

89

lathe which were glued to a piece of cloth or canvas; it was possible to make this work on a track so that the tambour would disappear as it was opened. Sometimes a cylinder front was incorporated. Here an entire section of wood, cylindrical in shape, would disappear when the piece was opened. The breakfront form became more popular and often had a central writing compartment. These are sometimes called 'Salem secretaries' because of the large number made in that city.

Chair backs began to reflect the increasing popularity of the classical style. Shield and heart backs became standard forms, as did square and oval backs. The great delicacy of some of these pieces makes them appear to have been created for show rather than for

Louis XVI style, classical, Philadelphia, painted white and gold, c. 1800. *Philadelphia Museum of Art*

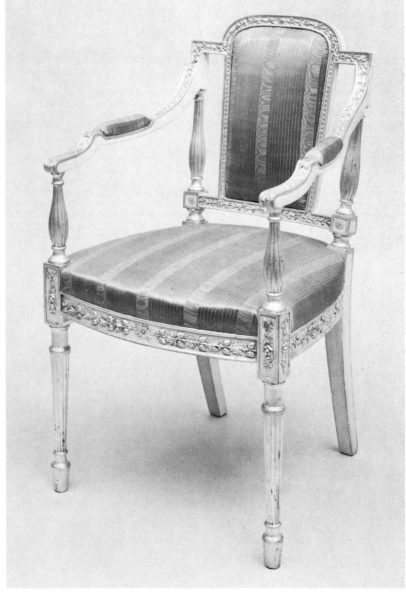

Cabriole arm chair
classical, Philadelphia, painted white and gold, c. 1800.
Philadelphia Museum of Art

actual use. Chairs and sofas also reflected the influence of the Louis XVI, see opposite. While these are rare, there seems to have been a taste for them in Philadelphia, as a group survive which were made there. The Martha Washington chair is a development of the time, see below. It is an outgrowth of the wing chair with upholstered back and seat and open arms. Another original American form of the period is the banjo shape for clock cases which Simon Willard patented in 1802, see page 92. Looking glasses were pedimented and decorated with urns and sprays or they incorporated églomisé or other panels painted with scenes or decorative motifs under a cornice with ball pendants, see page 92.

Easy chair
classical, Philadelphia, mahogany, 1805–1815. *The Henry F. duPont Winterthur Museum*

Martha Washington arm chair
classical, Massachusetts, Dorchester, stamp of Stephen Badlam, mahogany, c. 1795. *The Henry F. duPont Winterthur Museum*

Looking glass
classical, Albany, pine carved and
gilded, c. 1810. *Albany Institute of
Art*

(right)
Wall clock
classical,
Massachusetts,
Roxbury, made by
Simon Willard,
mahogany painted,
1802–1810. *The
Henry F. duPont
Winterthur Museum*

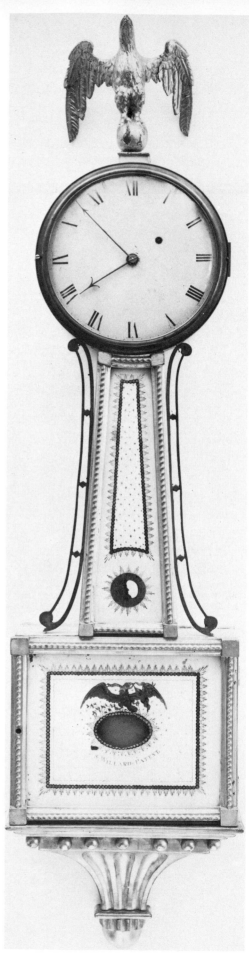

(above)
Overmantel looking glass
classical, New York or Albany,
white pine with gesso and gold
leaf, c. 1805. *The Henry F. duPont
Winterthur Museum*

(below left)
Cylinder-fall desk and bookcase
classical, possibly Maryland,
mahogany inlaid with various
woods, 1790–1800. *The Henry F.
duPont Winterthur Museum*

(below right)
Gentleman's secretary
classical, Salem, labeled by
Nehemiah Adams, mahogany
veneer and white pine, 1795–1798.
*The Henry F. duPont Winterthur
Museum*

Regional characteristics became less pronounced
during the classical era. However, some did linger so
that recognition of given areas is still possible in many
instances. New England furniture still remained the
most conservative and was conceived in a highly
delicate manner, see page 94. It was only here that
stretchers were retained to connect chair legs. The
heart- and shield-shape backs were popular for chairs;
Salem chairs often had a large urn as a splat with festoons radiating from it and the rear legs had an
inward curve near the bottom. The bow-front
chest, with contrasts of light and dark veneers, was a
typical form, along with the dressing table (with
attached looking glass) and the breakfront.

Rhode Island cabinetmakers developed a type of
chair back which is characteristic. The shield-shaped
back is centered by a flattened Greek urn or dish called

a *kylix*. Another example of this type of chair, in the Karolik collection at the Boston Museum, has carving by Samuel McIntire and is thought to have been made in Salem. Rhode Island card tables often have a tapering geometric inlay on the legs which is surmounted by a small 'book' inlay.

Connecticut furniture continued to be fashioned of cherry, while mahogany universally remained the favorite wood of the period in other areas. Connecticut classical furniture is characterized by the elaboration of its inlays. A pattern of wavy lines resembling the pinwheel was favored, along with bellflowers with 'dot' outlines, 'carrot' inlays and eagles with shields. As in earlier periods, this furniture has a certain naïveté and originality of proportion which gives it a unique appearance.

The quarter-fan inlay is so often encountered in New York work that it has become identified with this school, although it is seen in furniture made in New Jersey. New York chair backs are square and have elongated urns as splats or inlaid Prince-of-

(below, left to right)
Shield-back side chair
classical, Rhode Island, mahogany, 1790–1800. *Museum of Fine Arts, Boston*

Square-back arm chair
classical, New York, mahogany, c. 1790–1810. *Museum of Fine Arts, Boston*

Settee
classical, Baltimore, attributed to Hugh and John Finlay, painted gilt and polychrome decoration, 1800–1810. *The Baltimore Museum of Art*

(opposite far right)
Lady's cabinet and writing table
classical, Baltimore, mahogany inlaid with satinwood, 1795–1810. *The Henry F. duPont Winterthur Museum*

Wales feathers. The latter is one of the most beautiful and intricate types of chair produced in classical America, see opposite.

The square-back chair was also popular in Philadelphia. Here it was given a characteristic urn and drapery treatment, or the back urns were intersected by vertical balusters. Painted chairs were another form of highly elegant furniture made in Philadelphia. In 1796, Elias Hasket Derby, the successful Salem merchant, ordered a set of 24 painted chairs with oval backs and Prince-of-Wales feather decoration through Joseph Anthony and Company of Philadelphia, see page 103. In this set there are three variants and they have been widely scattered among a number of collections. The sophistication of the decoration and its reliance on English motifs possibly suggests an English decorator. Sideboards with round ends were also a speciality of Philadelphia cabinetmakers.

Baltimore became an important port in the years immediately following the Revolution. A school of cabinet making began to flourish there which was to

produce some very elaborate examples of painted furniture, see page 95. Parts of several sets of seat furniture and tables have survived, which have surfaces painted with views of famous houses from Baltimore and its environs. A settee at the Baltimore Museum is signed by both Thomas Renshaw, who made it, and John Barnhart, who decorated it. This type of painted furniture is unique as a group and differs from that made in any other part of the United States. Also typical of the Baltimore school is the use of églomisé glass panels with allegorical figures. Large ovals inlaid in mitred panels are a characteristic of this school. The carving of the bellflower on Baltimore

Card table
classical, Baltimore, attributed to Hugh and John Finlay, painted gilt and polychrome decoration, 1800–1810. *The Baltimore Museum of Art*

furniture is also unique. Each petal is carefully delineated so that it is apart from all others.

Little documentary evidence exists about furniture made south of Baltimore during the classical period. Itinerant cabinetmakers and joiners continued to go from plantation to plantation in Virginia and the Carolinas, see page 110. In Charleston, a distinct type of carving is seen which is called 'rice carving', because it resembles the ripe grain of that plant. Furniture continued to be imported by Southern cities from Europe as well as from other parts of the United States. This might possibly explain the strong affinities between a chair with a long Charleston history and New York classical chairs. This chair is presently preserved in the Museum of Early Southern Decorative Arts (Winston Salem, North Carolina), and it was originally made for the Ball family of Charleston, c. 1800.

A considerable amount is known about classical cabinetmakers, because a number of pieces have survived with labels, brands, or other documentation. Charles Montgomery's excellent recent work *American Furniture, The Federal Period* (New York, 1966) deals with the great collection of classical furniture at the Winterthur Museum. The book illustrates all the labels from pieces in the collection and provides brief biographies of the cabinetmakers represented.

The Boston-Salem area produced some superb furniture during the period. The Seymour family is probably foremost along with Samuel McIntire in that area. John Seymour (c. 1738–1818) arrived in Boston c. 1794 from Portland, Maine, and it is assumed that he had only just arrived in Portland from England. His son Thomas (1771–1848) was associated with him from c. 1800, but it is believed that the father designed and constructed most of the furniture. Their work sometimes bears an identifying label 'John Seymour & Son' and also a characteristic robin's-egg blue paint on compartment interiors. Tambour construction was brought to masterful height through inlaid decoration by the Seymours and their inlay on pilasters is unique. In 1805 Thomas was listed alone in the Boston directory and in this year he offered upholstering among his services. One of the Seymour masterpieces is the commode in the Karolik collection at the Boston Museum, made of mahogany, satinwood, bird's-eye maple, and rosewood, between 1790–1800, see page 100. It was sold in

Girandole looking glass
classical, probably Boston, pine with gesso and gilt, c. 1800–1810. *Museum of Fine Arts, Boston*

Arm chair
classical, Boston, attributed to John and Thomas Seymour, mahogany, c. 1795 *Museum of Fine Arts, Boston*

Deer Park parlor
Baltimore County, Maryland,
c. 1800. The secretary-bookcase is
attributed to the shop of John and
Thomas Seymour. *The American
Museum in Britain*

Baltimore dining room
c. 1810. Baltimore elegance is
shown in the delicate classical
furniture, accented by the ceiling
height. *The Metropolitan Museum
of Art*

1809 to Elizabeth Derby of Salem by Thomas
Seymour, although it was probably made by his
father. Radiants on its top are inlaid in alternating
woods; they converge at the rear in a small semi-
circular area which is painted with sea shells. It is
thought that John R. Penniman of Boston did the
painting. The piece is further embellished with lions'
head brasses and brass paw feet. Identical brasses are
seen on other Salem pieces and the brass paw feet on
documented pieces by the New York cabinetmaker
Duncan Phyfe.

Samuel McIntire (1757–1811) is remembered, not
only as a furniture carver, but also as a designer of
important buildings and a carver of architectural trim,
see page 111. He came from a family of carvers, and
came into prominence in 1782 as the architect and
builder of the Peirce-Nicholas house in Salem. In 1800
he was employed by Elias Hasket Derby to design
and build a house for his daughter Elizabeth West at

Chest of drawers
Chippendale, Connecticut, made by
Kneeland Adams, cherry, 1793.
*The Henry F. duPont Winterthur
Museum*

Commode
classical, Boston, made by Thomas
Seymour with painting by John
Penniman, mahogany, satinwood,
bird's eye maple and rosewood,
1809. *Museum of Fine Arts, Boston*

Wine cooler
classical, Boston, attributed to John and Thomas Seymour, mahogany and satinwood, c. 1795. *Museum of Fine Arts, Boston*

Sofa
classical, Salem, carving attributed to Samuel McIntire, mahogany, c. 1800. *Houston Museum of Fine Arts*

Peabody, Massachusetts. He worked on Oak Hill, as the house was called, during 1801 and 1802. Even after his death his son Samuel Field (1780–1819) continued to repair and change the house. In all, McIntire designed 20 houses in Salem and it is fortunate that not one of them was destroyed in the fire of 1914 which razed most of the city. In a sense, he closely resembled Robert Adam in his involvement with architecture, interior detail and furnishings. Of the documented pieces of furniture that survive there seems to be a greater preponderance of sofas and chairs. Motifs used on this furniture were close to those used in connection with houses that he built.

Favorites among these were a basket of fruit and flowers, a sheaf of wheat, alternating fluting with rosette, eagles, husks in pendants, a cornucopia, a bunch of grapes, an urn with festoons and flowers and laurel wreaths. Most of the attributed pieces are in mahogany, but bird's-eye maple and satinwood were also used. Sofas were of two general types—square and round back—and chairs followed the same trend. Sometimes the carved ornamentation is set against a background created by a snowflake punch. Among the books listed in the inventory of McIntire's estate are volumes on architecture by Palladio, Ware, Langley, and Paine. His son, Samuel Field, did competent work but it in no way had the originality of his father's work.

Nathan Hawley and Family
by William Wilkie, watercolor,
November 3, 1801. A rare survival,
this watercolor provides
documentary evidence of the actual
appearance of a turn-of-the-19th
century room. *Albany Institute of
History and Art*

NATHAN HAWLEY, and FAMILY, Nov. 3. 1801

Drawing room
Harrison Gray Otis House, Boston,
1795. The house from which this
richly Adamesque room comes was
probably designed by Charles
Bulfinch. *Society for the Preservation
of New England Antiquities*

Side chair
Philadelphia, 1796. Made of painted beech, this oval-back chair is one of a set of 24 ordered by Elias Hasket Derby of Salem, Massachusetts through his agents Joseph Anthony and Co. of Philadelphia. *Museum of Fine Arts, Boston*

Stenciled bedroom
Joshua La Salle House, Windham, Connecticut, c. 1830. Simplified furnishings in the classical style are shown in this room from a country house. *The American Museum in Britain*

A Salem cabinetmaker whose work was once confused with that of McIntire was Nehemiah Adams (1769–1840). His work is characterized by long bulbous feet and table legs have a long cylindrical neck and heads at the top and bottom. This is also a general characteristic of Salem furniture. Nathaniel Appleton, Sr (active 1803) of the same city was exporting furniture in the early years of the 19th century. Edmund Johnson (active 1793–1811), was an important Salem cabinetmaker. He produced furniture of fine quality, chiefly for export. It is obvious that much of his furniture was intended for the South and he is recorded as having accompanied shipments there. William Hook (1777–1867) worked with Johnson as well as Jacob Sanderson. Characteristic of his work are carved water leaves on capitols crowning corner columns. These have a distinctive quality because of an undulating outline surmounting each of the leaves. It is possible that Hook worked with Nehemiah Adams, for the elongated bulbous feet characteristic of Adams' work are sometimes found on pieces made by Hook. Elijah Sanderson (1752–1825) and his brother Jacob Sanderson (1758–1810) worked together in Salem from 1779 until 1820. They were also in the export business and their shop employed many workmen. An important bed in the Pingree House, Salem, is by Jacob Sanderson.

John Doggett (died 1857) of Roxbury, Massachusetts, was a cabinetmaker, carver and gilder. He is chiefly remembered for the cornices on a bed in one of the McIntire rooms at the Boston Museum, which he gilded for William Lemon (Salem, active 1796) their maker. Doggett had a furniture factory and employed a number of workmen to perform individual tasks. Joseph Short (1771–1819) of Newburyport, Massachusetts, is remembered today principally because of the so-called Martha Washington chairs he produced.

Newport is not remembered as an important cabinetmaking center during the classical period. Stephen Goddard (1764–1804) and Thomas Goddard (1765–1858), were sons of John Goddard. Several labeled pieces by them in the classical taste survive. John Townsend (1732–1809), who has been discussed previously, also made some pieces in this later style. Holmes Weaver (1769–1848) was advertising in Newport as early as 1799. A labeled pembroke table which bears his label is in the Karolik collection,

Boston Museum. It has inlays of satinwood and rosewood on the legs and the satinwood is decorated with engraved design. The work of Adam S. Coe (1782–1862), also of Newport, is an interesting example of the conservatism in New England furniture. A labeled mahogany sofa by him in the Winterthur Museum is in the Chippendale style.

The Chapin family of Connecticut continued to make furniture into the classical period. Aaron Chapin (1753–1838) of Hartford had made pieces in the Chippendale style with his second cousin Eliphalet, but after his move to Hartford in 1783, his work began to show classical influence. A documented

Sideboard
classical, New York, mahogany with inlay, c. 1795. *Sleepy Hollow Restorations*

sideboard survives at the Wadsworth Atheneum, Hartford, which he made for Frederick Robbins of Rocky Hill. A bill dated 1802 exists; the piece described is made of mahogany rather than the usual cherry. Lemuel Adams (active 1792), was also working in Hartford. He was a partner of Samuel Kneeland (1755–1828) from 1792 to 1795. Adams made furniture for the State House, completed in 1796, and two years later was advertising cherry furniture. Kneeland made looking glasses in addition to furniture. Silas Cheney (1776–1821) had a cabinet shop in Litchfield. He kept careful account books between 1799 and 1821 and through the descriptions given, it is possible to identify a number of pieces made by him. Cheney seems to have specialized in sideboards and one exists in the Judge Topping Reeve House in Litchfield which is listed in the account book for September, 1800.

(above)
White Hall dining room
Near Charleston, South Carolina,
1818. Furniture from Baltimore,
Virginia and South Carolina graces
this room with its elegant classical
proportions. *Museum of Early
Southern Decorative Arts*

(right)
**Dining room of the Perry
Plantation House**
Summerville, South Carolina, 1806.
The early phase of classicism is
demonstrated in every detail from
this room. *The Brooklyn Museum*

(opposite)
Desk and bookcase
Baltimore or Philadelphia, c. 1811.
This mahogany piece represents the
height of style in America classical
furniture. *The Metropolitan Museum
of Art*

Fire screen desk
classical, New York, mahogany
with inlay, c. 1795. *Sleepy Hollow
Restorations*

Drop leaf table
classical, New York, mahogany,
c. 1810. *The Metropolitan Museum
of Art*

New York City became highly important in the shaping of taste in the United States shortly after the Revolution. Several cabinet-makers who had migrated from Europe settled in New York and made considerable impact on furniture design. Probably one of the most famous names associated with American cabinetmaking, Duncan Phyfe (1768–1854) began work in New York at this time, see page 115. Born in Scotland, Phyfe first lived in Albany, but is recorded in New York directories by 1792 where his name was spelled 'Fife'. By 1794 the spelling had been changed. Phyfe carried on the business under his own name until 1837 when it became Duncan Phyfe & Sons. In 1840 it was changed to Duncan Phyfe & Son and remained this way until he disbanded the firm. By 1847 he retired, after accumulating a sizeable fortune, and sold his remaining stock at auction.

When Phyfe began cabinetmaking in New York, he favored the designs of Sheraton, although slightly later he was to come under the influence of French Directoire design. The rich mahogany from Cuba and Santo Domingo was favored for his furniture; instead of using contrasting woods, he used carefully cut veneered panels for dramatic effects. Rosewood became a favorite in his shop after 1830.

Phyfe was one of the first American cabinetmakers to successfully incorporate the 'factory' method into the workings of his shop. He employed cabinet-makers with journeymen and apprentices as well as carvers, turners, and upholsterers. Because of the division of labor which was involved, it is more proper to refer to the 'school' or 'workshop' of Duncan Phyfe rather than to attribute furniture directly to him. Furniture made in the workshop was expensive. A bill dated 1816 from Phyfe to Charles N. Bancker of Philadelphia (preserved at the Winterthur Museum) lists the prices of an elaborate suite. Mahogany chairs are listed here at $22.00 and a sofa at $122.00.

Two different labels were used on Phyfe's furniture. The earlier reads 'D. Phyfe's Cabinet Warehouse, No. 35 Partition (S)treet New York, and the other gives his address at 170 Fulton Street. Favorite decorative motifs were the lyre, acanthus leaf, plume, cornucopia, drapery, laurel, wheat ear, thunderbolt, bow knot, trumpet, harp, and rosettes. Reeding is to be seen universally in this furniture, and it is contracted from top to bottom on a tapered surface.

Brass pulls as well as brass feet were used. The repertory of Phyfe's work in the early classical style includes virtually every category of furniture, combining delicate classical motifs in an entirely original manner.

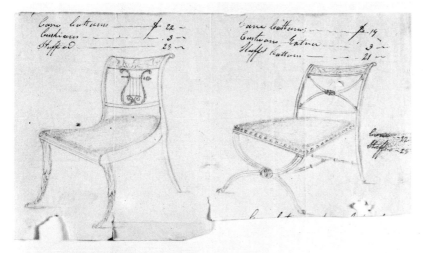

Drawing of chairs, with estimate
Sent by Duncan Phyfe to Charles N. Bancker of Philadelphia in 1816. *The Henry F. duPont Winterthur Museum*

Piano
classical, New York, made by John Geib, mahogany, 1815–1819. *The Henry F. duPont Winterthur Museum*

Piedmont Room
Guilford County, North Carolina,
c. 1766. The furniture shown here
reflects the time lag in style which
itinerant southern craftsmen
perpetuated. The stretcher table
probably dates from no earlier than
1770 and furniture of this type
continued to be made into the 19th
century. *Museum of Early Southern
Decorative Arts*

The Dinner Party
by Henry Sargent, oil, co. 1820.
This and a companion piece, *The
Tea Party*, provides a glimpse into
Boston life in the early 19th
century. *Museum of Fine Arts,
Boston*

(left)
Dining Room of the Irvington, New Jersey House
c. 1820. A dependence on the actual appearance of antique furniture models is seen in this room. *The Brooklyn Museum*

(below)
The McIntire Room
Chimney-piece by Robert Welford of Philadelphia. This setting displays the finest furniture of the period c. 1790–1810. All the chairs reflect the style of Samuel McIntire of Salem. *The Henry F. duPont Winterthur Museum*

Card table
French Restoration type, New York,
mahogany with brass mounts and
trim, c. 1825. *The Metropolitan
Museum of Art*

Pier table
classical, New York, mahogany
with marble top, c. 1815. *The
Metropolitan Museum of Art*

Settee
classical, New York, attributed to
Duncan Phyfe, mahogany,
c.1815–1825. *The American
Museum in Britain, Bath*

Several cabinetmakers working in New York at the time were producing furniture of a very high quality. For many years a gaming table at the Museum of the City of New York was attributed to Phyfe, until the stamp of Lannuier was found on the edge of a drawer. Charles Honoré Lannuier (1779–1819) arrived in New York from France with two brothers in the 1790s, see opposite. It is possible that he worked in Phyfe's shop on arrival and this would explain the close resemblance between their furniture. He established his own shop and employed another Frenchman,

John Gruez, as foreman. His early work is in the Sheraton and Directoire styles but, like Phyfe, he eventually embraced archaeological classicism. Lannuier used two labels—a simple printed one and another which was elaborately engraved. Both of these were in English and French. There is an important gaming table at the Winterthur Museum which is labeled, as well as the example at the Museum of the City of New York.

(above)
Pier table
classical, New York, stamp of Charles Honoré Lannuier, mahogany, brass and marble, 1805–1810. *The Henry F. duPont Winterthur Museum*

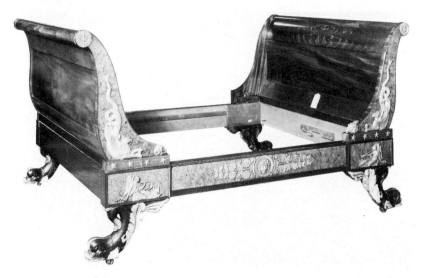

(left)
Bed
classical, New York, stamped Charles Honoré Lannuier, c. 1817. *Albany Institute of History and Art*

Michael Allison (working 1800–1845) is a cabinetmaker whose work has also been attributed mistakenly to Phyfe. Elbert Anderson (working 1789–1800) was another maker of superior ability. An end of a three-part dining table can be seen at Van Cortlandt Manor, Croton-on-Hudson, New York which bears his label, which was engraved by Cornelius Tiebout. John Budd (active 1817–1840), was another New York maker in the same tradition, who exported furniture to the south. Two cabinetmaking partnerships were active at the time. One, Mills & Deming, is first mentioned in the directory for 1793, and they are mentioned as late as 1798. Several documented and labeled pieces which survive show they were excellent craftsmen. The other partnership, Slover and Taylor (active 1802–1804), produced a distinct type of chair and sofa with a square back which had a half daisy carved in the cresting piece. A final mention should be made of New York looking glass makers. William Wilmerding (active 1785–1794) emigrated from Germany and a number of looking glasses survive which bear his label. Charles, Joseph and John Del Vecchio were active 1801–1844 and two types of labels survive which they used.

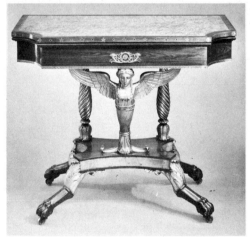

Card table
classical, New York, attributed to Charles Honoré Lannuier, mahogany, maple and gilt, c. 1815. *The Metropolitan Museum of Art*

113

(above)
The Chillman parlor
Assembled room to show furniture
of the period 1815–1840.
Archaeological classicism is to be
seen in all the furniture shown.
Pieces were made in Philadelphia
and New York and many are the
work of French cabinetmakers who
migrated to those cities. *Houston
Museum of Fine Arts*

(right)
Ideal Interior
Andrew Jackson Davis, watercolor
1845. Davis worked as an architect
in both the classic and Gothic
styles. This is a plan for a parlor in
the severe Roman style. *The New
York Historical Society*

Side chair
Baltimore, 1815–30. One of a set of nine, this chair is an archaeological version of the *klismos* shape. *The Metropolitan Museum of Art*

(below)
Group of parlor furniture
New York, mahogany with linen and wool upholstery, 1837. Tradition states that this furniture was ordered by Samuel A. Foot, a New York lawyer, from Duncan Phyfe. *The Metropolitan Museum of Art*

Arm chair
classical, Philadelphia attributed to
Ephraim Haines, mahogany,
c. 1790. *Philadelphia Museum of
Art*

Two cabinetmakers who worked in northern New Jersey at this time clearly demonstrated that, in some areas, furniture in a number of styles was being produced simultaneously. Matthew Egerton, Sr (died 1802) of Brunswick, New Jersey, was of English ancestry, although his wife had Dutch forebears. His oval pasted paper label has been found on a number of pieces and on this basis it has been possible to attribute a number of other pieces to him. The label reads Matthew Egerton, Cabinetmaker in Burnet Street, New Brunswick (NJ). He worked with veneers in the classical style and although the exteriors of his pieces are always masterfully executed, the interiors sometimes betray workmanship which is not so careful. Evidence would indicate that secretaries, bookcases, tables, clock cases, chests, beds and other case pieces were his specialty; in other words, he probably did not make chairs. While he was making furniture in this fashionable manner, his shop was also producing the much earlier *kas* form. Here, Dutch baroque influence, which had reached its height of popularity at the turn of the 18th century, was still to be seen. It is obvious that the settlers of northern New Jersey, many of them of Dutch background, still had a taste for this kind of furniture.

Matthew, Jr (died 1837) owned his own shop in New Brunswick as early as 1785. The earliest marked example of his work is a tall grandfather clock with his pasted label inside the door. It reads 'MADE and SOLD by Matthew Egerton, Junior, Joiner and Cabinetmaker, New Brunswick, New Jersey—No —' Two types of labels were used: the earlier was octagonal in shape and the later was scalloped along the edge. The son's work is so similar to that of his father that it can safely be assumed he was apprenticed to him. In some instances the work is so similar that it is virtually impossible to distinguish the work of the father from the son. Matthew Jr had two sons, one of whom, Evert, was in partnership with his father for a period. They used the firm name 'Matthew Egerton (Jr) & Son'.

The chief cabinetmakers associated with Philadelphia during this period were Ephraim Haines (1775—died after 1811) and Henry Connelly (1770–1826) see opposite. Haines had been apprenticed to Daniel Trotter and his first works were in a simplified Chippendale style. Between 1806 and 1807 Haines made a set of ebony chairs for Stephen Girard. In style, his furniture is delicate, chair backs are square with vertical turned balusters and the feet flare in a bulbous manner. Connelly's furniture is quite similar and the shape of the foot is often the only distinguishing characteristic. Both of these cabinetmakers use an oak-leaf type of acanthus carving. The Philadelphia Museum owns a fine documented group of furniture by these cabinetmakers, as does Girard College.

John Aitken (active 1775) was born in Scotland but migrated to Philadelphia at about the time of the Revolution. He made the famous tambour secretary-bookcase for President Washington when he retired to Mount Vernon. The secretary, which cost $145.00, is preserved at Mount Vernon. At the same time he made a number of other pieces for the Washington family. These included two side tables, a desk and a set of 12 chairs with square backs, of which the latter are in the collection of the Smithsonian Institution. Aitken has been described as Washington's favorite cabinetmaker.

As Baltimore was a thriving metropolis, it is only natural that a number of cabinetmakers would settle there. The sophistication and grace of much of the production of this school can hardly be matched by any other area. Unfortunately, little information of a documentary nature has come to light concerning Baltimore cabinet-makers. Stitcher and Clemmens (active 1804) are listed in the Baltimore directories and a mahogany secretary made 1795–1810, which is in the collection of the Baltimore Museum, has the following pasted paper label: 'Stitcher & Clemmens, Cabinet and Chair Makers Corner of South and Water-Streets, Baltimore. Orders from the city or country attended to with punctuality. They have St. Domingo Mahogany of the best quality for sale.' In the lower section of the secretary are four oval panels with satinwood outlines which are set into mitred panels.

Painted furniture was a specialty of the Baltimore school. The settee (mentioned earlier) at the Baltimore Museum, decorated with romantic and fanciful scenes, is imprinted 'Thos Renshaw, No 32 S. Gay St. Balti. John Barnhart Ornamenter'. From this, it may be assumed that Renshaw was the cabinetmaker and Barnhart did the decorations. Renshaw is listed in directories for 1814 and 1815. John and Hugh Finlay (active 1799–1833) were also chiefly noted for their painted furniture. However, in 1803 and 1804

Side chair
classical, Philadelphia, attributed to Ephraim Haines, mahogany, c. 1790. *The American Museum in Britain, Bath*

Side chair
classical, Philadelphia, attributed to Henry Connelly, mahogany, c. 1790. *Philadelphia Museum of Art*

Family of Joseph Moore
Erastus Salisbury Field, oil, c. 1840.
The family is shown with a late
classical serving table and stenciled
chairs of the Hitchcock variety.
Museum of Fine Arts, Boston

(right)
Dining room
Lyndhurst, Tarrytown, New York,
1839. A. J. Davis designed the
house in two stages in the Gothic
style. *The National Trust for
Historic Preservation*

(opposite above)
Parlor, the Robert Milligan house
Saratoga, New York, 1853. The
furnishings show the opulent
rococo-revival style. *The Brooklyn
Museum*

(opposite below) see page 120

they made marble-top corner tables, a pier table and a pier glass. It was probably one of these brothers who executed the set of furniture, from the 1808 designs of the architect Benjamin Henry Latrobe, for the President's House in Washington.

This set of furniture was destroyed in the burning of the President's House during the War of 1812. On exhibition at the Baltimore Museum is a set of furniture made by the Finlays for John B. Morris. It consists of two settees, 10 chairs, and a pier table. This set of furniture is decorated with views of the homes of famous Baltimorians of the period. The recent publication of William Vose Elder's *Baltimore Painted Furniture* (Baltimore, 1972), throws new light on this furniture. Mr. Elder lists cabinetmakers from directories and provides all the latest information available on this important American contribution to cabinetmaking.

Annapolis became another Maryland cabinetmaking center. John Shaw (1745–1829) was an important maker there and a considerable amount of documentary evidence about him survives. Shaw was apparently trained in England and first arrived in Annapolis in 1773 with a partner, Archibald Chisholm. This partnership was dissolved in 1776. The most famous label to be found on Shaw's furniture is octagonal with 'John Shaw, Cabinetmaker, Annapolis' in the center surrounded by a wreath and a small oval at the top with 13 stars. Shaw was selected to make the furniture for the House of Delegates of the new State House. Examples of Shaw's work are preserved at St. John's College, Annapolis, the Maryland Historical Society and the Baltimore Museum of Art. Shaw's furniture displays certain individual characteristics. He used blocked feet on most of his pieces and a characteristic type of oval panel inlay which is never perfect in its execution. Little is known about furniture which was produced in this style south of Maryland.

In Europe, classicism began to move into a new stage at the very end of the 18th century. Classical archaeology became more and more absorbing for intellectuals and designers. Recent findings revealed the actual appearance of Greek and Roman furniture. Sources were chiefly wall and vase paintings, for only a few actual antique pieces of furniture had been found. A taste developed to reproduce the life of classical times—to live and dress as the Greeks or

Side chair
Curule base, classical, New York, attributed to Duncan Phyfe, mahogany, 1810–1815. *The Henry F. duPont Winterthur Museum*

(page 119, below)
Mrs Martha J. Lamb Seated in Her Library
by Cornelia A. Fassett, oil, 1878. One of the earliest Americans to write on the decorative arts of her country. *The New-York Historical Society*

120

Romans. Therefore, modern versions of classical furniture were needed. Several antique forms came to be associated with the new Græco-Roman furniture. The *klismos* chair was formed by a solid horizontal cresting piece at the top with legs flaring outward in saber shape; usually a decorative slat ornamented the form see page 115. The *curule* is a chair or bench form which has an X-shaped support that meets the seat and supports the piece from the floor, see opposite. The throne and tripod censer were also classical forms which were imitated.

The archaeological forms were codified by two French designers, Charles Percier and Pierre F. L. Fontaine. They published an elaborate collection of plates *Recueil de Decorations Interieures . . .* in 1801 with a second edition in 1812. It was these designers who were chosen by Napoleon Bonaparte as official court architects and decorators, when he established his Empire, in 1804. Because of this, the term 'Empire' has long been associated with this archaeological-classical phase. Typical Græco-Roman motifs were acanthus leaves, cornucopias, swans, eagles, dolphins, and monopodia (combination of animal leg and head together without the body). The furniture was rectilinear, massive, and heavy and was enriched with gilt bronze mounts; mahogany and rosewood were favorite woods. Napoleon's Egyptian campaign carried back elements from this antique source to be included in the design vocabulary. The lotus, hawk, sphinx, and hieroglyphics were often used on forms which were essentially Græco-Roman, as little was known at the time about the actual appearance of Egyptian furniture. After the Bourbon Restoration (1814–1830) in France, the overall shapes of the Empire style were retained. Restoration and Charles X furniture still had the classical lines of the earlier style but the decorative surface detail was missing from it and fruitwoods replaced mahogany in popularity. The gondola chair, a variant on the *klismos* form, was popular during the Restoration and Louis Philippe (1830–1848) periods.

This phase of classicism became very popular in England, where it was known as the Regency style. Sheraton's late works *The Cabinet-Maker and Upholsterer's Drawing Book* (1802) and *Designs for Household Furniture* (published after his death in 1802) begin to show the introduction of Græco-Roman forms. Thomas Hope, a friend of Percier, published *House-*

Side chair
Klismos type, classical, New York, attributed to Duncan Phyfe, mahogany. 1810–1820. *Henry Ford Museum*

(opposite)
New Orleans bedroom
Shown in an idealized setting, this enormous mahogany bed is attributed to Prudent Mallard of New Orleans. In the transitional rococo-Renaissance revival style, it is made of mahogany. *The American Museum in Britain*

(right)
A Window, House on Hudson River
by Worthington Whittridge, oil, 1863. Furniture of several popular French revival styles is seen in this room. *The New-York Historical Society*

hold *Furniture and Interior Decoration* in 1807. An antiquarian and collector, Hope liberally borrowed from the *Recueil* in creating his designs. Another element of the English Regency style which must be considered is the taste for the exotic and picturesque; Chinese and Hindu designs and motifs became popular and were often superimposed on rather regular classical furniture forms. An interesting mixture of this taste with the classical can be seen at the Brighton Pavilion, which was built for the Prince of Wales in 1815 by John Nash and decorated by Frederick Crace.

A trend away from archaeological exactness began to be seen in England in George Smith's publication of *A Collection of Designs for Household Furniture and Interior Decoration* (1808). The furniture shown was heavy, bulbous, and architectural, but it lost the precise flavor of its predecessors. In a second work *The Cabinet Maker and Upholsterer's Guide* (1826) a further debasement can be observed. Heavy columns, with capitals in all the classical orders and winged lion's paw feet, began to appear. This popularisation can be traced in Rudolph Ackermann's *Repository of Arts, Literature, Fashions, etc.*, a periodical which appeared between 1809 and 1829. The greatest

(above)
Center table
classical, Philadelphia, labeled by
Antoine-Gabriel Quervelle,
mahogany with gilt and inlaid
marble. *The Metropolitan Museum
of Art*

(right)
Sofa
classical, Boston, made by William
Hancock, mahogany, 1826–1828.
The Metropolitan Museum of Art

Side chair
Klismos type, Boston, branded by
Samuel Gragg, birch and oak,
1808–1815. *The Henry F. duPont
Winterthur Museum*

general work which related to the style was John
Claudius Loudon's *Encyclopedia of Cottage, Farm and
Villa Architecture and Furniture* (1833, with many
succeeding editions). This was a kind of everyman's
guide which included simple examples of this
debased furniture. The popularization and debasing
of classical furniture forms was to last as a major
trend in Europe until the end of the second quarter of
the 19th century. By this time, only certain architectural elements and proportions remain to remind
one of the original source of inspiration.

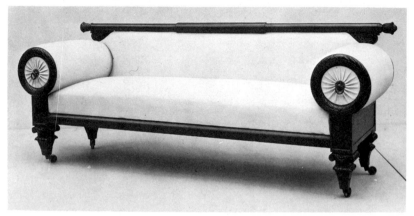

In the United States, Duncan Phyfe used saber legs
on *klismos* or Grecian chairs as early as 1807 and, at
about the same date, introduced the *curule* form for
chair and settee bases and benches, see page 120. Lyres,
eagles and other devices were introduced into the
backs of chairs. Phyfe's career continued through the
archaeological period into the late 1830s and 1840s.
At this time his factory was turning out heavy, plain
furniture in the debased classical style. A famous set
of furniture made by Phyfe in 1837 for Samuel A.
Foot of New York is in this style, and is in the collection of the American Wing, Metropolitan Museum,
see page 115. Because of Lannuier's early death in
1819, his work did not develop to this late type. He
did produce furniture in the most severe and correct
Empire manner; a generous use of ormolu mounts
typifies this period in his work. Figures carved as
parts of Lannuier's furniture have a naturalistic
quality, see page 113. A. G. Quervelle, another French
emigré, produced elaborate furniture in the archaeological taste in Philadelphia.

Sheraton fancy chairs, as they were called, began
to be produced in great numbers in the first quarter of
the century. Related in form and decoration to the
painted furniture made in such areas as Baltimore,

Side chair
Connecticut, Hitchcocksville, made by Lambert Hichcock, light wood painted and stenciled, 1825–1828. *Henry Ford Museum*

Sewing table
Shaker, New Lebanon, New York, pine, c. 1850. *Hancock Shaker Village*

these chairs were more mass-produced. They were of light construction and generally had rush or cane seats. At times the cresting piece would be decorated with a romantic scene while at others, the back would be formed into a single device such as a shield or an eagle. A Boston cabinetmaker, S. Gragg, made remarkable chairs c. 1815, see opposite. They were a variant of the *klismos* shape, with the outline from the front seat rail to the cresting composed of a piece of bent hickory, while oak was used in other parts. They were painted a solid color and decorated with peacock feathers or flowers and often branded with the maker's name.

Lambert Hitchcock (1795–1852) at Hitchcocksville, Connecticut (today called Riverton) began the manufacture of a type of chair which was to make his name famous. This chair was an early example of mass production. Several types were made but the characteristics remained the same. Frames were generally made of birch or maple with a broad curved member at the top, a wide curved slat and a cross-piece below. The stiles are continuations of the legs; the front legs and lower stretchers are turned. Seats of rush, and later plank, were wider at the front than the back; the chairs were made to sell for $1·50 retail. They were marked on the back of the seat with the stencil 'L. Hitchcock, Hitchcocksville, Connecticut, Warrented'. It was the stenciled decorations in bright colors that made these chairs especially popular. All went well for Hitchcock until 1829 when he was forced into bankruptcy and the business was transferred to others.

At the same time, a religious sect, the Shakers, had developed a distinct type of furniture which was essentially based on classical lines, see page 128. The founders of the sect had reached America in 1774 and by the early years of the 19th century had established communities in various parts of New England, New York State, Kentucky, and Ohio. Shaker furniture is totally utilitarian and is stripped of ornamentation. It continued to be made into the 20th century, by which time it had become stereotyped and banal.

In the mainstream of furniture production, the influence of Smith's *Guide* was felt in the United States as early as 1830. Ornate columns began to appear on case furniture and the winged lion's paw became increasingly popular. Stenciled decoration was also popular on city-made furniture. One of the most

(above)
Not at Home
by Eastman Johnson, oil, c. 1875.
The cluttered furnishings typifies
Renaissance revival-style tastes.
The Brooklyn Museum

(opposite)
Cabinet
Charles Tisch, New York, 1884.
Inlaid rosewood cabinet.
The Metropolitan Museum of Art

Shaker Room
The furniture seen here was made at Shaker settlements in Hancock, Massachusetts and New Lebanon, New York, between 1810 and 1850.
The American Museum in Britain, Bath

important firms in the dissemination of this phase of classicism was Joseph Meeks and Sons (1797–1868) of New York. They had a large furniture factory and warehouse which was shown in a lithographic broadside printed by Endicott and Semett in 1833. In addition, it showed 41 pieces of furniture and two sets of draperies. It is of considerable importance, for it is the first American publication to show complete furniture design. The broadside shows pieces with projecting columns and a considerable use of C and S scrolls. The massive architectural quality of this furniture is virtually all that is left of the classical influence.

In 1840, the first book of furniture designs produced in the United States was published in Baltimore. It was John Hall's *The Cabinet Maker's Assistant*. Hall believed the elliptical curve to be the most beautiful single element in design and the 198 plates in the *Assistant* reflect this feeling. C and S scrolls are combined in every conceivable manner; Hall believed that anyone who was proficient with a band saw could make furniture after his patterns. Because of the

Side chair
French Restoration type, New York, mahogany, c. 1830. *The Metropolitan Museum of Art*

Voltaire chair
French Restoration type, New York, mahogany, c. 1835. *Sleepy Hollow Restorations*

Wardrobe
classical, New York, mahogany with stenciled decoration, c. 1830–1835. *Museum of the City of New York*

heavy columns used on case pieces and the variety of scrolls, this type of furniture is popularly called 'pillar and scroll'. It shows a strong influence from the furniture of the French Restoration style. Late debased classical forms continued to be popular into the 1850s. The great American mid-century tastemaker Andrew Jackson Downing (1815–1852) showed classical furniture, which he called 'Grecian,' in his *Architecture of Country Houses* (New York, 1850). At that time he felt that it was still the most popular for private residences.

Thus American classicism has been traced from its beginnings with neoclassical motifs superimposed on relatively straightforward furniture forms, to its debasement about 75 years later. The entire movement was a continuum, with no specific beginning or end. For the sake of convenience, the phases might be dated as follows: neoclassicism, c. 1785—c. 1810; archaeological classicism, c. 1810—c. 1830; debased classicism, c. 1830—c. 1850. The classical influence did not end at this time and it has been felt, in one way or another, in furniture production ever since.

Other revival styles
1830–1900

It might be said that the main stream of taste during the 19th century was dominated by the revival of styles which had been popular in earlier times. As has been seen, the influence of Greece and Rome lasted for a considerable period. Simultaneous with their taste for the classical, designers were turning to other historical sources for inspiration. Whether it was the design of the Middle Ages, the Bourbon courts, or the Ottoman Empire, those involved with taste borrowed motifs and styles rather than developing original ones. In a sense, it might be said that Chippendale did the same thing, but it must be remembered that he combined motifs, which were often disparate, into original new forms. In some instances this happened with the 19th century revival styles, while in others there was a concerted effort actually to imitate or reproduce a complete furniture form from an earlier period.

The machine had become a dominant factor by this time. All aspects of the Industrial Revolution had come to influence the United States by the end of the first quarter of the century. While furniture 'factories' such as those of Phyfe or Allison had employed machinery and the assembly line technique, it was now (by 1825) possible to make most of the frame of a piece of furniture by machine. Because of this, in some instances the time honored pride in craftsmanship began to disappear in favor of mass production. Comfort became increasingly important; it was to influence the design of furniture and to increase the demand for elaborate upholstery. Many designers and furniture manufacturers of the 19th century believed they were making 'antique' furniture as their work was thought to follow the lines of earlier models so carefully. Any careful look will distinguish the 19th century work from its earlier model. Designers could not help but put something of themselves into their furniture, so that these works betray their time of origin.

The Gothic revival

Acorn clock
Gothic shape to face, Connecticut, Bristol, made by Jonathan Clark Brown, Forrestville Manufacturing Company, mahogany, 1847–1850.
Henry Ford Museum

The roots of the Gothic revival lay in England where the decorative vocabulary, especially architectural, of the Middle Ages had never completely disappeared. William Kent had applied Gothic as well as classical motifs to baroque furniture forms in the 17th century and Chippendale had contributed a number of designs to his *Director* (1754) which showed the Gothic influence. Horace Walpole used this style in the remodeling of his house Strawberry Hill (after 1747). While the style waned in popularity at the end of the 18th century, it reappeared in Smith's *Household Furniture* (1808) along with numerous pieces in the classical taste. These pieces applied Gothic architectural ornaments to furniture forms and in no way imitated actual Gothic furniture. Indeed, little was known at the time about the actual appearance of Gothic furniture.

Ackermann's *Repository* first included Gothic furniture designs in 1817. This serial publication also showed furniture designs by the medievalist Augustus Charles Pugin, which were collected in book form in 1827. His son, Augustus W. N. Pugin, published *Gothic Furniture in the Style of the Fifteenth Century* in 1835. The following year, a book was published in London which showed several medieval pieces; it was Henry Shaw's *Specimens of Ancient Furniture* and survives as the first book on English antique furniture.

The Gothic style was never as popular in the United States as in England. Somehow, it was associated with the church, and it was used chiefly in great houses designed by important architects. Much of the American furniture which survives—and there is little of it in comparison to the other revival styles was designed by architects for specific settings. Its chief architectural ingredients were the pointed and lancet arch, trefoil and quatrefoil rosettes, heraldic devices, crockets, finials, and tracery. Alexander Jackson Davis (1803–1892) was one of its chief American exponents; the furniture which he designed for Lyndhurst at Tarrytown, New York survives there today, see page 118. Arguably the most creative single group of Gothic revival furniture in the United States, much of it was possibly executed by the firm of Burns and Trainque of New York. John Jelliff (1813–1893) of Newark, New Jersey, produced furniture in this taste which is delicate and relies heavily on Gothic tracery for decoration. There is an excellent collection of Jelliff's furniture, as well as designs for it, in the Newark Museum.

Easy chair
Gothic revival, probably New York, walnut, c. 1850. *The Metropolitan Museum of Art*

The Elizabethan revival

Slipper chair
Elizabethan revival, rosewood, c. 1840. *Chicago Historical Society*

The Gothic style had first stirrings in the United States when it was incorporated into what were essentially classical forms. An English cabinetmaker and designer, Robert Conner, migrated to the United States and in 1842 published his *Cabinet Maker's Assistant* in New York. This survives as the first American design book of Gothic furniture; and it should be remembered that it came just two years after the publication of Hall's *Assistant*, which dealt with furniture in the debased classical style. Downing shows Gothic furniture in his 1850 *Architecture of Country Houses.* He recommends its use in the libraries of private houses as it carries with it the attribute of serious contemplation. Downing treated a number of the revival styles in this manner and assigned them to particular rooms according to their suitability.

In a sense, the Elizabethan style was closely related to the Gothic, for both largely relied for their effect on open-work surfaces and the play of light on these surfaces. Actually, 'Elizabethan' is a misnomer for this style, although it was so-called in the 19th century. Furniture in this style was made in the United States from c. 1835—c. 1855. Its actual source of design inspiration was the vocabulary of the eras of Charles I and II rather than of Elizabeth I. Baroque turnings with characteristic spiral and ball were the chief ingredients of the style and they go back to the designs of Daniel Marot. In England, both Smith and Ackermann included Elizabethan designs in their works,

Downing shows chairs in this style which have high backs and resemble the prie-Dieu form. It was a style particularly fitted to the execution of hall and slipper chairs and it most often was seen in these forms. The backs of these chairs could be completely open-work or they could have upholstered center sections. An important offshoot of the style was the production of a type known as cottage furniture. Actually, this was an inexpensive, mass-produced descendant of the painted furniture which had begun to be made in the last quarter of the 18th century and had found its way to being produced in a different form by Hitchcock. Cottage furniture was popular by the 1850s. It was made of a variety of types of cheap softwood which was then painted; split spindles were applied to the front of case pieces and ball and 'sausage' turnings were used on the legs of tables and chairs. Downing illustrates several sets of such furniture, which he admired because of its suitability to country houses, its practicality, and especially its inexpensive nature. It could be painted in a number of colors and often, in its floral and scroll decoration, announced the coming of another popular revival style, the rococo.

The rococo revival

The most universally popular furniture style in the United States from the 1840s through the end of the century was the rococo. Indeed, this style never ceased being made and there are factories today which produce machine-made rococo revival furniture. Its source of inspiration was the elegant style of the court of Louis XV; its chief ingredients included the cabriole leg, shell and other fanciful carving, curved surfaces and a profuse use of S and C scrolls. Curved lines had never totally disappeared from the design repertory, so in this sense it was not a revival but an exaggerated continuation. The style was popular in Paris and London as early as c. 1840 and numerous design books appeared in both cities which showed fanciful and elaborate variations on it.

It is not difficult to distinguish this furniture from its 18th century design source. Lines are heavier, the cabriole leg loses its delicacy and sometimes terminates in an S scroll toe, and at others in a cylindrical manner. The rear leg is chamfered at its termination to give a sense of solidity. The elaborate scrolls are interpreted in a heavy manner and naturalistic carving of birds, fruit, human busts, flowers, etc., is included. The cost of furniture of this type depended on the amount of carving on it and the least expensive was carved with simple 'finger' scrolls, see page 135. Walnut was a favorite wood for inexpensive pieces of rococo furniture while rosewood was reserved for the more expensive. It was possible to produce furniture of this type completely by machine, so it was widely disseminated across the country. Parlor sets were often executed in the rococo style, with a sofa, arm and side chairs, although all forms were made in it, see page 119.

Downing was fond of the 'French Antique' style, as he called it, particularly for use in parlors and boudoirs. In *Country Houses*, (1850) Downing illustrates three side chairs in this style, of which one had straight turned legs. This foreshadows the short-lived Louis XIV style of the 1860s. Samuel S. Sloan's

Arm chair
Rococo revival, New York, possibly by John Henry Belter, laminated rosewood, c. 1855. *The Metropolitan Museum of Art*

Homestead Architecture (Philadelphia, 1867) contained a valuable section relating to furniture in which the author honestly confessed to being confused by the design terminology assigned to different styles. However, he showed sets of seat furniture which relate to the design of most of the Bourbon courts.

Certainly the most famous figure connected with the American rococo revival is John Henry Belter (1804–1863), see page 133. It might be said that he succeeded Phyfe as New York's most fashionable cabinetmaker. Belter was born in Germany and served his apprenticeship in Würtemberg where he was trained as both cabinetmaker and carver. He was working in New York by 1844 and occupied several shops, the last on Third Avenue at 76th Street where he employed as many as 40 apprentices. The firm was called J. H. Belter & Co. from 1856, when several brothers-in-law joined him. He hired carvers trained in the Black Forest or Alsace-Lorraine because of the excellence of their work. Belter is known to have destroyed most of his patterns and pattern molds before his death. The firm continued to operate after his death until it finally became bankrupt in 1867.

Belter's chief contribution to the history of cabinetmaking lies in the technological innovation which he used in constructing his pieces. It would be very difficult to achieve the complex and lacy effects of Belter's furniture if solid pieces of wood were used. Although it would probably be possible to carve a chair back, for instance, from a solid plank of board, the grain would have to be perfectly suited to the design. Therefore, Belter introduced the process of lamination or the gluing together of thin layers of wood (rosewood, oak, ebonized hardwood, about $\frac{1}{16}$ inch thick) so that the grain of a given layer ran in opposition to that on either side. In general, the layers varied from six to eight, but it sometimes varied from three to 16. The laminated panels were then steamed under great pressure in molds or 'cawls', as he called them, so that undulating lines could be achieved. When extra ornament was needed, carved pieces were glued on.

There was considerable stylistic change in Belter's work during his career. The furniture was rather loose in form in the late 1840s and early 1850s when a strong Louis XV statement was made. He achieved a tighter form from the mid 1850s until his death, when the Louis XIV, Louis XVI and Renaissance styles became

Stool
Exotic antique revival, New York, labeled by Alexander Roux, wood elaborately painted, c. 1865. *The Metropolitan Museum of Art*

Sofa
Louis XVI revival, New York,
attributed to Leon Marcotte, black
wood and gilt metal trim, c. 1860.
The Metropolitan Museum of Art

Child's bed
Renaissance revival, made by
Alexander Roux, rosewood,
c. 1848–1866. *Museum of the City of
New York*

Balloon-back side chair
Rococo revival, mahogany veneer
on walnut, c. 1855. *Sleepy Hollow
Restorations*

popular and were reflected in his work. Some early pieces have backs constructed entirely of scrolls. This design was modified so that scrolls enclosed an area which was dominated by naturalistic carving. It is in the high backs of slipper and hall chairs that some of the greatest virtuosity of Belter's work is to be seen. In these, scrolls are combined with naturalistic detail such as flower, fruit and vine motifs. Later, the scrolls were to disappear and the backs were formed completely of naturalistic detail. When the Louis XVI taste became popular, Belter's furniture assumed a more balanced form. Belter applied for several patents on his laminating and steaming processes. This was a period when the Patent Records office in Washington was being besieged by cabinetmakers with specific patents. The Renaissance taste was to be interpreted by Belter in seat furniture and in a specially patented bed, an example of which can be seen at the Brooklyn Museum.

For many years all elaborate laminated rosewood furniture was called 'Belter'. However, an important manuscript notebook, by another New York cabinetmaker, Ernest Hagen, came to light and gave new information on this matter; the notebook is now in the library of the Winterthur Museum. It tells of the infringement which another New York cabinetmaker, Charles H. Baudoine (active 1845–1900) made on Belter's patents. This was done simply by running a seam down the center of a chair back rather than by forming the back from a single panel. It is now known that other cabinetmakers used lamination and steaming but the exact identification of their work needs further study. There was apparently a circle of cabinetmakers working especially in New York, who produced this superbly fashioned furniture.

There were many other cabinetmakers working in the rococo style. The Meeks Brothers continued to work in New York in this style, as did Gustave Herter, Leon Marcotte and Alexander Roux; in Philadelphia there were George Henkels, Daniel Pabst and Gottlieb Volmer; in New Orleans Francois Seignoret and Prudent Mallard; and S. S. Johns in Cincinnati. These cabinetmakers chiefly used mahogany, rosewood, and walnut, although painted lightwood was used for simpler pieces. New forms which evolved at the time were the etageré or 'what-not', the balloon-back chair, shown left, the single-end sofa, which was derived from a classical form, the méridien, and the sofa with high ends and a low center section.

A sub-style of the rococo previously mentioned was the Louis XIV. It was not popular, possibly because it was generally quite massive and clumsy. The 'Louis Quatorze' style, as it was called, was generally reserved for case pieces and incorporated such design motifs as heroic figures, broken-arch pediments, geometric detail, and naturalistic garlands. Great sideboards made in this style seem to drip flowers, fruit and trophies of dead game.

Historical revivalism c. 1865–c. 1900

During the third quarter of the century, New York continued to be America's taste and design center. Across the country, the best in cabinetmaking, carving, and upholstery was being executed by immigrant or visiting French and German craftsmen. These cabinetmakers began to vie with one another for novelty in production. By this time it was not unusual to combine elements from different revival styles into a single piece. Thus, trends towards eclectism began to be seen.

The Louis XVI style enjoyed a certain popularity in the 1860s. Its source of inspiration apparently lies in the 1850s in Paris when Empress Eugenie had the private apartments of the Tuileries and St Cloud restored. As she identified herself with Marie Antoinette, it is only natural that she should have chosen this style for the redecoration. Paris became a great center for the manufacture of this furniture, often embellished with porcelain plaques, and it was imported at New York.

Native American pieces are characterized by the use of oval backs and straight stiles, arm supports, and legs. A black or ebonized finish was the most popular and mahogany a favorite wood. Ormolu mounts were used and could be in the shape of bow knots or classical medallions; other classical motifs were inlaid of mother-of-pearl, ebony and holly. Some of the most elaborate American pieces also incorporated porcelain plaques. This furniture continued to be made through the 1880s and into the 20th century; and the later examples often bear closer resemblance to the original models. New York was a center for making this furniture, where such firms as Leon Marcotte, Thomas Brooks, the Sypher firm and Christian and

Arm chair
Renaissance revival, Meriden, Connecticut, rosewood, c. 1870.
The Metropolitan Museum of Art

Tall case clock
Oriental influence, New York, made by Tiffany and Company, mahogany, c. 1885. *The Metropolitan Museum of Art*

Gustav Herter supplied the wealthy. It is important to note that firms such as these did upholstering, drapery making and actively engaged in interior decorating. In other words, it would not be unusual to engage such a firm to decorate a room or house and to supply all the furniture. Jelliff of Newark and Henkels of Philadelphia also made Louis XVI furniture.

Another style, the Renaissance revival, became popular during the second half of the century, see pages 122, 126. Its exact source has not yet been discovered but it is mentioned by writers before 1850 and, in that year, was referred to by Downing. It is characterized by massive, square, architectural forms, with a use of broken-arch pediments, applied medallions, acorn trim, and tapering baluster-turned legs. G. Hunzinger of New York produced some of the most sensitive furniture in the style. He was German and was working in New York by the 1860s as he patented a folding chair in 1866. The folding mechanism must have had a profound influence, for most of his stationary seat pieces look as if they should fold. His work was delicate, for the style, and it shows a mastery of the design vocabulary. Other important makers of Renaissance furniture were John Jelliff of Newark, Daniel Pabst of Philadelphia, and Thomas Brooks of Brooklyn. The style was popularized for the entire nation through its mass production at Grand Rapids. Here, such a company as Berkey & Gay made quantities of Renaissance style furniture which was shipped to every part of America.

During the 1890s, a new vogue developed—the collecting of antique furniture and decorative items. Clarence Cook in his *The House Beautiful* (New York) as early as 1878 had described a collector who had furnished his city and country house in 'Antique American or English'—it apparently made no difference—furniture that he had bought in the country. By 1897, Edith Wharton and Ogden Codman, Jr in their book *The Decoration of Houses* were advising Americans to turn themselves to Europe for inspired taste, especially to Renaissance Italy and France. Miss Wharton's complete contempt for the American 19th century was shown in the *Age of Innocence* (1920) when she wrote of 'the purest 1830, with a grim harmony of cabbage-rose-garlanded carpet, rosewood consoles, round-arched fireplace with black marble mantels and immense glazed bookcases of mahogany.'

137

Side chair
Renaissance revival, New York, stamped by George Hunzinger, walnut, 1869 (dated). *The Metropolitan Museum of Art*

Especially popular 'antiques' were associated with Spain, Italy, France, and the Orient. Interest in America's past was fanned by the Philadelphia Centennial Exposition, in which one small exhibition was given over to a New England colonial kitchen. After the exhibition Americans became interested in their past, increasingly, and then reproductions of 17th century, Queen Anne, Chippendale, and eventually Chinese furniture began to be made. This furniture was once popularly called 'Centennial', but there is no evidence to show that any of it was shown or indeed made at the time of the exhibition.

Orientalism grew in popularity toward the end of the century. It was essentially Near Eastern in its inspiration, but motifs from a number of design vocabularies were combined, see page 137. At its most advanced, the taste found outlets in such extravagant expressions as the smoking room for the Rockefeller house at 4 West 54th Street in New York City. The entire architectural setting and contents of the room were made and put together by a decorating firm c. 1885. Moorish design dominates the whole and the furniture relies more on upholstery than frame for comfort and decorative detail. The room may be seen at the Brooklyn Museum. In houses of lesser pretension, the 'Turkish corner' became popular. This was a confection of Oriental rugs, pillows, tent-like drapery, teakwood screens, Koran stands, smoking equipment and, invariably, palms or other exotic plants. The cabinetmaker's art tended to disappear under the tufting, fringes and tassels of the upholsterer. The coil spring was generally combined into the construction of this furniture.

By the end of the century, 'eclectic' was the key word to be applied to American furniture. Much was produced by machine and even so-called 'custom-built' pieces were created in this way. At the same time, great architectural firms were purveying a related taste. The influential firm of McKim, Mead and White dominated New York taste in the 1890s. The very rich were by this time completely under the domination of European taste; such a house as Cornelius Vanderbilt's The Breakers, designed in 1892 by William Morris Hunt, was filled with European 'antiques'. Some of these pieces were indeed antique, while others were made in the furniture 'factories', particularly those factories in Italy, from which they were exported in great numbers.

Innovation and reform 1850–1914

(top)
Settee
Rococo revival, cast iron, c. 1850.
Sleepy Hollow Restorations

(above)
Settee
Gothic and rococo revivals, cast
iron, c. 1850. *Sleepy Hollow
Restorations*

At the same time that revivalism seemed to dominate taste, some designers were experimenting with technical innovations which could be combined into furniture forms and with new materials for making furniture. Belter has been mentioned for his re-introduction of laminated wood panels. This was of importance because it gave furniture greater strength and provided a medium for shaping and elaborate carving. A designer who experimented with lamination and bending by steam was the Austrian, Michael Thonet (1796–1871). By 1850 he had perfected a process for bending straight dowels of birch wood into highly elaborate designs. The influence of the rococo revival style is seen in his work, but his construction method reduced the elements of a furniture form to basics. Thonet's product, known as 'bentwood', enjoyed a wide popularity. It was shipped to this country in pieces and assembled with screws in the salesroom. Chairs and settees generally had seats and backs which were composed of caned panels. Thonet patented his furniture, but there were imitators in the United States.

A material which was not produced in great amounts in the United States, but which was important in 19th century furniture design, was papier-mâché. It was made by pressing together under great pressure paper pulp or strips of paper with glue. When the molded piece had set, it was taken from the mold and treated with successive coats of heavy paint or lacquer. It was decorated with paintings and inlaid with nacré. Because of technological advances in steam-driven presses, it was possible to make large pieces of furniture by this method. English and French factories exported this furniture and other decorative accessories to the United States and papier-mâché became a popular elegancy by the mid-century. An attempt was made by the Litchfield Manufacturing Company (Connecticut) from 1850 until 1854 to make papier-mâché, but a few serving stands survive as the only furniture produced.

Metals were also used for furniture making, and

Moose horn chair
owned by President Theodore
Roosevelt, c. 1870. *Sagamore Hill,
Oyster Bay*

Elk horn chair
photograph by Matthew Brady,
dated 1864. *Smithsonian Institution*

cast iron was most popular. The iron industry had developed more efficient methods of molding which made possible the production of larger single units, see page 139. Great numbers of cast iron chairs, settees, and tables intended for garden use, as well as umbrella stands and hat trees for interiors, were produced. The units of these pieces were shipped unassembled, and were fashioned into complete furniture forms by the seller. Factories which produced iron furniture also generally made pieces from heavy wire, which was twisted into highly fanciful shapes. Furniture of hollow steel tubes were being made in France during the 1840s, and in England by the 1850s of brass. Generally rockers were made and a bent section of the metal tubing formed the entire rear member of the piece. An American variant survives, of similar design, in which flattened iron elements were substituted for the tubes. It is a chair thought to have been made between 1850 and 1860 by Peter Cooper (1791–1883) at his iron foundry in Trenton, New Jersey.

An important innovation was furniture which incorporated a mechanical device. Comfort was ever-important and designers tried to achieve it in highly imaginative ways. As early as 1840, in his *Assistant*, Hall had shown a chair which could be converted into a day bed. From the middle of the century, the Patent Office in Washington was flooded by inventions for folding, dual or triple purpose, and convertible furniture. Closely aligned with this was the care given to dentists' and barbers' chairs, and built-in furniture for railroads and steamships. Elaborate pieces of cabinet furniture were patented because of their ingenuity in concealing pigeon-holes and storage compartments; Wooten Brothers in 1874 patented one of the most complex of these. The metal coil spring came into common use in the second half of the century. A notable American product, illustrated in the catalogue of the Crystal Palace Exhibition of 1851, was a centripetal spring chair which was patented by the American Chair Company of Troy, New York. This chair had a spring installed in the connecting section between base and seat so that the chair would recline when the seated person pushed against its back. The frame was of cast iron and often upholstered in plush carpet. Coil springs were extravagantly used in Turkish frame chairs of the 1880s and the 1890s; The frame was of iron or steel with all other parts made up

Bed
Oriental influence, probably New York, maple simulated as bamboo, c. 1880. *The Metropolitan Museum of Art*

of coil springs. Wooden elements were only to be found in the legs and their connecting members. Such pieces were elaborately upholstered.

While technological progress was producing innovative furniture, another type was being made completely by hand. This was furniture made from organic materials and intended for picturesque settings. One of the simplest was made from natural tree branches. Two articles of Downing's, posthumously published in his periodical *The Horticulturist* in 1858, described the methods of making furniture from rustic wood. Closely related was furniture made of cane (wicker or rattan). It was a durable tendril from an Oriental climbing palm and was imported into the United States. Gervase Wheeler, writing in his *Rural Homes* (1852), describes the magnitude of the industry in New York. The cane was soaked in water and then woven around frames which were fashioned from hickory or white oak. Bamboo was also imported and made into seat furniture, tables and cabinets and pieces of pseudo-Japanese lacquer were set into them to heighten the Oriental feeling. Pieces made of pseudo-bamboo were also popular, see above. Wood was turned to look like bamboo in these. An unusual type of organic furniture was made from the horns of native animals, see opposite. The great interest in the American West during the second half of the century brought this furniture to be popular. The horns of deer, antelope, buffalo, steers, etc., were made into seat furniture and tables. Chairs and settees were sometimes upholstered in the skin of the animal from which the horns had come, or in a plush fabric.

Reform

Side chair
Arts and Crafts, Chicago, designed by George W. Maher, 1897. *Park District of Oak Park, Illinois*

As early as 1850 in England, there was an outcry against the excesses of taste which were produced by revivalism and the increased use of the machine. Leaders like Henry Cole, Owen Jones, and John Ruskin were focal in the inception and continuation of the movement. William Morris (1834–1896) also became involved through his belief that good design could come only through a return to the hand methods of the Middle Ages. He and his associates embraced many crafts, among them furniture making, in the 1860s, but the handmade and painted furniture which they produced proved too costly for popular consumption. Another advocate of good taste in the Morris manner was Charles J. Eastlake. His book *Hints on Household Taste* was first printed in New York in 1872 and was to influence taste through the remainder of the century. He was against revivalism and advocated a return to simple English Gothic ornament. Many of his decorative devices and furniture forms can be seen in extant pieces but it is almost impossible to duplicate a piece from a plate in his book.

All this interest in design reform in England culminated in the founding of the Arts and Crafts Movement which flourished from c. 1882 until c. 1910. Workmen banded together in guilds where hand work and proper use of materials were emphasized. Cottage furniture, stripped of ornamentation and utilitarian in character, was idealized by this movement. In the United States, the reaction to revivalism could be found in the furniture produced by the Boston architect Henry Hobson Richardson (1838–1886). While principally known as an architect working in the Romanesque taste, he began to design furniture in the early 1880s for public buildings, which reflected Eastlakian ideas. Oak was the favorite wood for this furniture, which was of Windsor and mortise construction and was essentially massive and rugged in line. He also incorporated Byzantine ornament into a few pieces which he made. The Boston firm of Irving and Casson and Davenport executed his designs.

When Richardson passed from the scene, a minority of Chicago and Pacific coast architect-designers carried on the tradition of design reform. Louis Sullivan (1856–1924) and Frank Lloyd Wright (1869–1959) had a great influence on Chicago's furniture manufacturers through their concept of simple masses

(opposite page, top)
Desk
Art Furniture or Eastlake, New York, made by Herter Brothers, ebonized cherry, 1877–1882. *The Metropolitan Museum of Art*

(right)
Design for table, chairs and top
Frank Lloyd Wright for Midway Gardens, Chicago, 1914. From *The Drawings of Frank Lloyd Wright*, Horizon Press, New York, 1962

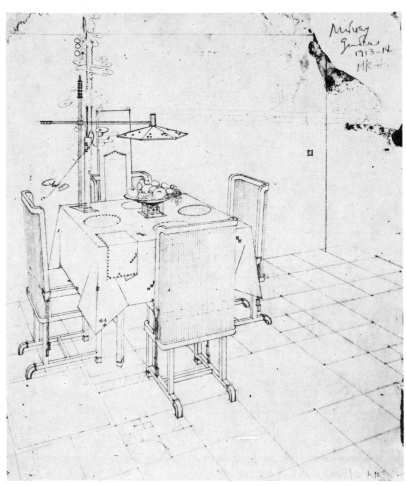

(below)
Table
New York, Tiffany Glass and Decorating Company, 1890–1905. *The Metropolitan Museum of Art*

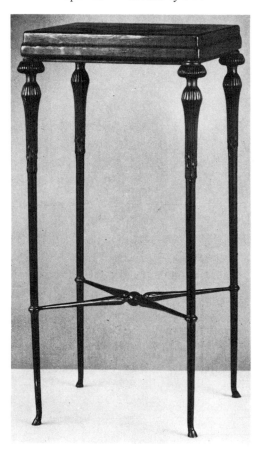

decorated only by a small amount of integrated organic ornament, see page 143. The Tabey Furniture Company was the leading Chicago firm of the 1890s. Wright designed furniture at the time which actually anticipated the Squared Craftsman-style furniture which was to follow. In 1904, Wright designed a movable metal chair with some rounded lines for the Larkin Building in Buffalo and in 1905 an armchair whose design was reduced to a cube.

Gustav Stickley (1858–1942) of Eastwood, New York, had formulated his own ideas covering Craftsman furniture as early as 1900. This furniture was made of oak in square lines and had visible mortise joints with upholstery and table tops made of brown leather or green canvas. These functional forms were to create what was eventually known as the Mission Style, whose name conceived the 'mission' for which the furniture was intended. His forms were imitated

Arm chair
New York, Tiffany Glass and
Decorating Company, maple with
marquetry decoration, 1890–1900.
The Metropolitan Museum of Art

Curio cabinet
Art Nouveau, New York, made by
George C. Flint, mahogany, c. 1910.
The Metropolitan Museum of Art

by Elbert G. Hubbard (1856–1915) of East Aurora, New York, who founded a communal society there which was an interesting outgrowth of the Arts and Crafts Movement. Printing and bookmaking were primary interests of the group but furniture highly derivative of Stickley was also produced. The Pasadena architects Charles and Henry Greene were in correspondence with Stickley and recommended his furniture for their clients who could afford it. They also designed highly sophisticated furniture of the same type. They, like Wright, had been profoundly impressed at the Chicago Fair of 1893 by the Japanese Pavilion, with its great truth and simplicity of form.

Mention should be made of the influence of Art Nouveau on American furniture design. While the other decorative arts were profoundly affected by this turn-of-the century movement, furniture was little influenced. The chief practitioner of the style was Louis Comfort Tiffany (1848–1933), and Art Nouveau design is best exemplified by the glass which he and his associates produced. His firm, Tiffany Studios, produced some furniture between 1890 and 1905 which showed a naturalistic influence through the inclusion of organic carving. The more ordinary furniture produced by Tiffany's firm was in the classical taste. However, the exaggerated whiplash curve and undulating organic surfaces which typified French furniture of the day, with which Tiffany was familiar, are not to be found. An eccentric exception is a cabinet by George C. Flint and Company of New York which was made between 1909 and 1913, see page 144. It awkwardly shows the influence of sophisticated French designers and is in the collection of the American Wing, Metropolitan Museum.

It was probably through innovative furniture and the work of design reformers that America made its chief contributions to furniture design. In the 20th century design became more universal with the Bauhaun tradition dominant. A brief examination of 20th century innovations will show that most have roots in the 19th century. American furniture of the 17th and 18th centuries was original in the sense that it combined European style elements in an essentially unique manner. The break with tradition began around the middle of the 19th century and the most original furniture production of the United States dates from after this time.